Poochie's
Changing Daze

Poochie's
Changing Daze

BEVERLY ANN MARCOUX JOHNSTON

iUniverse, Inc.
Bloomington

POOCHIE'S CHANGING DAZE

iUniverse books may be ordered through booksellers or by contacting:

iUniverse
1663 Liberty Drive
Bloomington, IN 47403
www.iuniverse.com
1-800-Authors (1-800-288-4677)

Because of the dynamic nature of the Internet, any web addresses or links contained in this book may have changed since publication and may no longer be valid. The views expressed in this work are solely those of the author and do not necessarily reflect the views of the publisher, and the publisher hereby disclaims any responsibility for them.

Any people depicted in stock imagery provided by Thinkstock are models, and such images are being used for illustrative purposes only.
Certain stock imagery © Thinkstock.

ISBN: 978-1-4697-7387-2 (sc)
ISBN: 978-1-4697-7389-6 (hc)
ISBN: 978-1-4697-7388-9 (ebk)

Printed in the United States of America

iUniverse rev. date: 05/15/2012

For Dalton and Sam
Memories of Mom

My Mother

You're just a babe
And your life is quite wild
Until you're all grown up
And no longer a child

You'll try to make
The best parts last
But get lost in the future
Forgetting the past

There are times to come
With decisions to make
New ropes to learn
And new turns to take

So don't get lost
In those sudden hopes
Just take all the turns
And learn all the ropes

In the times to come
You'll remember the pain
Only to find
You're beginning again.

—Poochie Marcoux

Contents

Acknowledgments

I'D LIKE TO THANK MY mother. She has taught me that patience and love are the keys to life. She is my soul mate. She is my rock, my hero, my saviour.

To my dad—you were a very important part of my childhood, and I never gave you enough credit for being the great father that you were and for being there always.

Thanks to Brian for being just the kind of brother I needed to make me who I am today. Your sarcasm and taunting taught me strength and tenacity.

Thanks to my sister, Brenda, for becoming my friend. You taught me to be strong, and to appreciate and learn from the lessons that life throws at me.

Thank you, Michelle, for holding my hand, making me laugh and being there for me.

To my loving husband, Scott—I thank you for your patience and understanding in allowing me to sit for hours typing and working on my first book. I love you for accepting me for who I am and for showing me that love can withstand anything.

Thank you to everyone who was a part of my past in the little town of Nairn Centre, Ontario, where I spent my childhood. There are so many great memories there for me. I miss the calm and easy life that came with growing up in a very small northern Ontario town. Nairn Centre, I salute you!

Prologue

1979

I'D HAD TO MAKE CHOICES, like whether or not to slit my wrists or take a bottle of pills. But I knew that ending my life would be a mistake. It was not the way to get out of things.

I was just tired of being tired. Sleeping all the time and waiting for time to pass, waiting to feel better.

I'd have to go back to school on Monday, and I needed to get prepared. We'd just returned from the cottage—Mom, Dad and I. We'd unpacked our things and settled back into the house.

I knew I had to start doing things, keeping myself busy, living my life again. It had been a difficult and painful summer. I had gotten through it, and I was going to be a better person for it.

Well, let's get started, I decided, and stood up from the edge of my bed.

I walked down the stairs to the doorway outside, slipped on my shoes and decided I was going to go out for a walk. I figured I'd go over to the general store and get some comfort food—an ice-cream cone, maybe.

I had opened the door just a crack when I heard the phone ringing upstairs. I left the door ajar and raced back upstairs, only to hear my father say into the receiver, "Sorry, you must have the wrong number. There's nobody that lives here by that name."

The person on the other end of the phone hung up. Dad hung up the receiver and went back to sit down in his La-Z-Boy chair.

I was disappointed. The phone calls were never for me anymore. I had turned back and started down the stairs again when I overheard my dad talking to my mom, who was sitting in the rocking chair crocheting a multicoloured afghan.

"What is Poochie's real name?" Dad asked Mom.

Mom looked up and out the window, paused for a bit and answered after a short hesitation, "It's Beverly."

"Oops, that phone call was for her," said Dad.

I heard him say that to Mom and stormed back into the living room, yelling, "Dad, you must know by now that my name is Beverly!"

"I'm sorry, I can never remember that name. You've always been Poochie to me. I'm sure that whoever she was will call back for you if it's important," Dad said.

"She," I asked, "not he?"

"No, Poochie, it was a girl on the phone," Dad replied. I sat down on the arm of my mom's rocking chair. Mom put her warm and wrinkled hand on my knee and gave it a rub.

"It'll be all right," Mom said. "You just need some time to go by, and you will find that this, too, shall pass." She laughed and added, "By the way, don't you think you're getting a little old to be sitting on the arm of my chair with me?"

"No, Mom, I'm never going to be too old. When the chair tips over, or the arm breaks off because I'm too heavy, then I'll consider it. But for now, I'm staying right here where I belong!" I said and hugged her.

Mom smiled and patted me on the knee. "You'll always be my girl, aye, Poochie?"

"Yep," I said. "Forever and always, Momma!"

Chapter 1

THE BEGINNING OF BABY WHO?

"WHY DID YOU CALL ME Poochie?" I asked my mom. It really bugged me that I didn't have a normal name.

Mom told me that after she had given birth to me, on December 5, 1962, she was in the hospital and a nurse came into her room. The nurse needed to know what the baby's name was going to be so she could put it on the birth certificate.

Mom said that she and Dad were not really set on a name yet.

When choosing names, my parents had one rule: to call all their children a name that started with a B. I had a brother, Brian, who was six years older, and a sister, Brenda, who was nine years older.

Mom and Dad had a few names—Bunny, Bonny, Barbara—rolling around in their minds, but they weren't terribly fond of any of those.

They figured that, when the time came, the proper name would just come to them. But there I was, in their arms, and they still didn't feel like they had a B name that they wanted to call me.

My mother had spent the last few hours in the hospital with a poor old lady in the bed beside her. Mom knew her from a long time ago when they were children. The lady was terribly ill and dying of cancer. She mentioned to my mom that she loved the name Beverly.

Mom and Dad had never heard of the name Beverly. They liked the sound of it and decided that it was a suitable name for me.

They brought me home from the hospital. Dad would be talking to me, and he couldn't remember the name they had given me. Mom found she was having a hard time remembering it too. So in their haste to give me a name they could remember, Poochie Pooh—Dad's pet name for me—was shortened to Poochie, and that's the name I was stuck with.

The name Beverly eventually got completely forgotten in our household.

When people would ask who I was, Mom, Brenda, Brian and Dad would all reply that my name was Poochie.

I can recall many times when they would look at each other, bewildered, waiting to see who would remember my real name. My dad never did.

Of course, my brother, Brian, had his own version of the story. Brian told me that Mom and Dad had really wanted a puppy. They were on their way to get a dog and Mom found herself pregnant with me, so they never got the dog because they couldn't afford a dog and a baby. I became a substitute for the dog they never had, and they called *me* Pooch instead.

"Everyone knew that you were a real disappointment and that Mom and Dad really wanted a dog," Brian exclaimed.

Chapter 2

GRADE 1

IT WAS 1967 AND I was lying on the red-and-white linoleum-tiled kitchen floor. It was a hot summer day and the floor was cold. Mom was beside me baking something scrumptious for dessert.

My feet were on the fridge, and I was swaying my body back and forth to feel the coolness of the floor against my back.

Suddenly, Mom was talking to me and telling me that I would soon have to start school. "Won't that be nice?" she said.

"I don't want to go to school!" I cried. "I want to stay here with you."

"No, no, no, there is no choice in the matter, Poochie," Mom said. "You have to go to school."

I would cry and pout whenever she would remind me. I hoped that all my tears would make some sort of a difference in her decision to make me go or not.

The day came when I had to go to school. Mom took me by the hand and walked me 25 steps from the front door of our house to the Nairn Public School, where I began my Grade 1 education.

Mom was holding on to me tightly by the arm because I wanted to run back home and stay there with her forever. I was not happy about having my life change from the way it was.

Papers had to be filled out, pictures had to be taken and immunizations had to be poked into me before they would even let me into a classroom. The process itself made me believe that school was going to be a horrible place that Mom was committing me to. I was going to have to stay there forever.

I wondered why Mom was punishing me. Why was I going to have to go to this place every single day for the rest of my life? Was Mom tired of me?

I thought to myself, *Why is she putting me here, and what will she do at home, the whole day, without me? We'll both just be lonely. I will get no time off to play, except when the people at the school say that I can!* I couldn't figure out what I did that was so wrong—wrong enough to make Mom want to leave me there all alone.

I was afraid I would become a clone, like all the other boys and girls who entered and left the place each day whenever the bell rang to say it was time to do so.

I cried and cried, and they had to pull my mother from me.

From the public school's Grade 1 window, I could see my house and my mother standing in the kitchen window doing dishes, cooking and baking, all by herself, without me.

Every now and then I would see Mom drive out of the driveway in our car. I would run to the classroom window, disturbed and distressed, and wonder where she was going without me.

If Mom was home when the recess bell rang, I would run home immediately and demand to know where she had been. This kind of behaviour got Mom's panties in a knot, and she had to give me a good talking to a few times.

I was not very happy for that first year, having to watch my mom come and go from our house. My dad started coming home early on occasion too. There was always something going on over there that I was missing out on.

The fact that I had my Grade 1 classroom on the side of the school that faced my house proved to be a real problem for my mother.

Somehow I got through the year, and with the other 30 kids who were in my Grade 1 class, I moved on to Grade 2. I got a new classroom, and it was on the other side of the school.

I forgot about the view of my house from the Grade 1 window. I stopped wondering what I might be missing out on at home.

I was better able to learn and function on the other side of the school. It was much easier to get through the day without the distraction of Mom and our house.

Chapter 3

CHOCOLATE CAKE

ONE DAY WE HAD A rummage sale at school. Most families donated things they didn't need or want at home anymore. There was a bake sale too, and all the moms baked and donated homemade goodies. My mom baked and brought stuff over the day before the event while I was in class.

During lunchtime on the day of the sale, my mom popped over and bought a bunch of Harlequin Romance pocketbooks. I was just coming out for recess and saw her, and before she left, she gave me some money to shop at the sale. After school, all the kids would have an opportunity to shop and buy things themselves.

I loved having money and going shopping. I went through the stuff at the rummage sale. It reminded me of when I was at the dump with Dad.

I bought some cookies and a Tupperware cake plate with a cover on it. I was so happy to see that I had just enough money left for it. I thought Mom could use it to store all the cakes and things she baked. It could sit on the counter and make a nice display with all of her handiwork.

Mom baked squares that were the best around, but her cakes were always kind of weird. I never really liked her chocolate cakes. They were always so dry we'd have to cover them with Carnation milk from a can to be able to eat them without choking.

When Brian and Dad and I would eat the chocolate cake, we would just gradually pour milk onto it, a little at a time, when Mom wasn't looking. We wanted to save Mom's feelings from being hurt.

We didn't want her thinking that we did not appreciate her hard work.

Eventually, even she admitted her chocolate cakes were a little dry. After that, we'd just mush the cake up with a fork and drown it with milk. Sometimes she would laugh and do the same, and sometimes she did not think it was very funny at all.

I brought the Tupperware cake plate home for Mom. I brought it into the house and kept it hidden behind me. I told her I had a great surprise for her, pulled the plate out from behind me and handed it to her.

She shrugged and looked at the cake plate like it was an old enemy that I never knew about. "I just gave that to the school yesterday for their rummage sale. I don't understand. Why would you go and buy it back?"

I was sad that she didn't like my gift, but I had no idea that it had been ours. I'd never even seen the plate before. I guess Mom never liked it, which was why she never used it.

I suppose it went into the dump after that, for some other treasure hunters to find.

Mom said that she did appreciate my thinking of her, and there was nothing lost and nothing gained from the sale.

Chapter 4

THREE TINY LIVES

"DAD PUTS ALL THOSE KITTENS into a paper bag and holds them against the exhaust pipe of the car," Brian said, trying to make me believe. "It kills them all by suffocating them with the gas fumes. You can hear them screaming and crying. When the kittens are all dead, he flushes them down the toilet." With an evil grin, he continued, "Dad has to get rid of them because they are going to grow up and be a nuisance. Menew will be next."

I sat on the floor looking down into the bloody box that Menew was lying in. Her kittens were gone.

"No . . . you're lying," I cried. "Dad doesn't kill them . . . he couldn't."

Our cat, Menew, had kittens in the middle of the night in my brother's room, in a cardboard box. I loved Menew, and I was pretty sure Brian did too. Brian often said things just to get my goat. I was sure this was one of those times.

I thought Brian was just being mean because he was tired and grumpy. The cat had kept him awake all night, crying through the birth of her kittens.

When I got up in the morning there were three of them—tiny, wet and sticky with blood, like little mice with kitten faces, crying and nuzzling beside their mom. They were all so adorable. I couldn't wait to get home from school to hold them, snuggle them and maybe wash them. I thought about them all day.

But where were they now? I ran to Dad.

"Brian's lying, right, Daddy? You did not kill the kittens, you couldn't, could you?"

Dad looked at Mom, Mom looked at me, and Dad walked out of the room without answering my question.

"Mom, no, it's not true, right?" I asked.

"Poochie, Brian is just saying that to bug you," she said as she shot Brian an angry look.

"Well, where are they then?" Brian opened his hands out in front of him, tapping his foot and directing his question at Mom.

Mom paused for a long time, looking at Brian like he had two heads or something, and then said, "Your dad and I brought them to the pound to get them adopted."

"You took them to the pound already? I never even got to see them or play with them," I cried.

"Dad and I didn't want Menew getting too attached to them. They had to go. We couldn't keep them all!" Mom explained.

"Couldn't we have kept just one of them?" I cried.

Mom hesitated. "Poochie, it's just the way things are, that's all! There's one too many cats here with Menew already." Mom didn't like cats, but I didn't believe she would lie to me.

Mom continued stirring the pot of boiling pasta that she was making for dinner. I walked away on that note. My brother was looking at me with a shit-eating grin on his face.

I hate Brian, I thought.

Chapter 5

BITING AND CHEWING

I SAT DOWN IN THE living room on the green shag-carpeted floor in front of the TV. My hands would just seem to rise up all by themselves. They would come up to my mouth, and I would start chewing the dry skin around my fingernails. By the time I'd realize how much I had eaten, my fingers were red and bleeding.

I asked everyone to try to help me stop biting my nails.

My mom bought me this yucky-tasting stuff—Stop and Grow, it was called. Mom would paint it on what was left of my nails, and it would make them taste bitter and awful. Everything that I touched that went into my mouth, including my food, ended up tasting like it too. I just became accustomed to it. I wondered if I should ask Mom for more when it had worn off and my food started tasting good again.

I couldn't stop biting. I'd start with the torn pieces of skin called hangnails. I felt I had to bite them off because the sharp edges would get caught on my clothes, sheets or towels. It hurt me when they got pulled. When I had bitten all the sharp little edges off, I would bite off all of the skin that was not smooth around my nail.

I figured that when all of the jagged skin pieces were gone, my fingers would stop hurting and they would be all smooth again. I suppose sometimes I got carried away.

My fingers would be raw and hurt really bad. It felt as though my skin was pulling away from the ends of my fingers, like the skin on each of my fingers were getting stretched too tightly.

I had everyone in the house remind me if I was biting my nails. But it got really annoying having them all after me and watching me all the time. I felt like I had to go and hide to do it so they wouldn't bug me anymore.

My brother was happy to help, offering to smack me every time he caught me biting. I thought maybe it would be a good way to make me stop, so I took Brian up on it. However, I soon realized he thought it was just a license to hit me. I almost had to find something to bribe him with to make him quit hitting me and pretending he was doing me a favour. Finally Mom told him to leave me alone.

I watched Menew cleaning her fur, licking and biting little things out of it. I figured that whatever was bugging her enough to bite them out of her fur like that must have been a real blessing to get rid of. I just concluded that my hangnails were the same for me.

I would distract myself from biting my nails by picking things—sometimes lint off clothes, little wool balls off my sweaters, little scratches on my skin. But never my nose like the dirty kids in town, and I never ate my scabs either. Yuck.

Chapter 6

FLANNELETTE AND RINGLETS

IN THE EVENING AFTER MY bath, Mom always had me wear flannelette pyjamas. Sometimes the PJs had feet in them, which I hated because they made me feel claustrophobic and hot.

Mom always had the first bath in the evening, and then I would have mine. We didn't have a lot of water, so I would use her bathwater when she was done. Brenda and Brian would get their own water because they were bigger and dirtier, I guess. Our water came from a well that we shared with the neighbours. We had to try not to use too much at a time, or the well would run dry and the neighbours would complain.

One time Mom left me to play in the tub. She'd just had a perfumed bath, adding an oil to her bathwater that smelled really nice. She said it would make me smell nice and make my skin feel really soft too.

When she returned to take me out of the bath, I was scratching and fussing around in the water with a mass of red hot bumps all over me. She quickly rinsed me off with warm water to get all of the perfumed water off of me.

I was very itchy all night. Mom said she guessed I was allergic to the perfume. I had always wanted to try everything that she used to make her smell so nice, but I thought I'd stick to the spray-on kind of perfume from then on. Even that sometimes caused me problems.

When Mom would use her musk perfume, if any would get on me, I would have to bathe right away because it would make my head pound with headaches. There were very few perfumes I could tolerate on my skin. I could spray them on my clothes, though, and they wouldn't bother me so much.

After getting me all pyjama'd up for bed, Mom would sit me down in front of her and brush my hair. She'd pull on the long, wet, tangled blonde hair and spray on No More Tangles to help make the knots slide out easier. I hated having my hair combed because it hurt. It was always so tangled and knotted. I always wondered why I couldn't just cut it off short. But Dad would insist, "Little girls have long hair, and little boys have short hair!"

My hair would be falling in my face and in my eyes. Dad finally decided that I should have some bangs cut into it.

I was so excited to be getting my haircut. My family never went to the hairdresser because Dad always figured that whatever someone else could do, he could do better.

Dad cut me some bangs; they were slanted across my forehead. He didn't cut them right. I was mad at him.

I remember all my school pictures having those crooked bangs. I thought maybe Dad knew something I didn't. By cutting the bangs all crooked like that, when I squinted in the mirror, the bangs looked kind of straight.

So maybe that's how I looked most of the time. I hoped so, anyway.

Nobody ever really said anything about my hair at school. I hated the fact that when the bangs would grow just long enough that no one could tell they weren't cut straight, Dad would catch me with the scissors and say it was time for another haircut. He'd cut the bangs and they would look all crooked again.

Mom sometimes would make rolls around her fingers with pieces of my hair and put bobby pins in to hold them through the night. I hated all those bobby pins sticking me in the head all night every time I moved.

Wednesday was laundry day. Mom hung all the clothes on the line after she'd washed them with the big wringer washer. She'd work hard pushing all the wet things through the wringer rollers to get the water out. It was a whole lot of work doing the laundry. Mom's hands would be red and sore at the end of the day.

Because she hung them on the line, the sheets smelled so good, but the towels were crunchy. My jeans would be so stiff they were like cardboard and could almost stand up by themselves. I hated the feel of my jeans; it almost hurt to bend my knees in them. When it was raining, Mom would use the electric dryer. The clothes were softer, but the smell wasn't the same. The electric dryer cost lots of money to use, so she only used it when she had to.

Mom would put flannelette sheets on my bed in the winter, and I hated them. With flannelette pyjamas and flannelette sheets together, I felt like I was Velcroed into my bed for the night.

Everyone in my family had a homemade quilt on his or her bed. Mom and Grandma made the quilts by hand. They would spend days at Grandma's house cutting the triangles and squares out of old shirts, jeans or corduroy pants that we had grown out of or damaged.

They would pin all the little triangles or squares with batting and sew them all together, one by one, with a needle and thread. Mom and Grandma would make quilts to use as gifts for friends and neighbours.

The bed covers were heavy when the quilts were made with old denim and corduroy pants. Sometimes it felt like you were lying under a big carpet.

If I took my quilt off my bed, I'd wake up with my thighs and calves aching. My legs always hurt when they got cold. I would have to tiptoe into Mom and Dad's room and wake Mom up. I'd tell Mom that I needed help because my legs were aching and I could not sleep.

Mom would get me a baby aspirin and put me back into bed. She'd cover me up with my quilt and tuck me back into my cocoon. I would feel better within half an hour after taking the aspirin. With my quilt back on top of me, I felt safe and secure again.

Mom told me that she got leg pains too sometimes, and it was arthritis. Lots of old people suffered with this arthritis stuff. I would see old women with their fingers all deformed, and I was told that it was arthritis. I imagined that someday it would be my legs that would be all mangled like that because that's where my arthritis was.

I'd have leg pain any time my legs got cold. If I sat on a cement step or played outside for too long in the spring or fall, I would hurt. I took a lot of baby aspirin because it was the only thing that would stop the ache.

Every morning, Mom would make me breakfast, either "muffetts"—big shredded-wheat balls poured under boiling water and then covered with milk and brown sugar—or toast with corn syrup on a plate for dipping. While I was eating, Mom would put my clothes out on the bed for me to wear to school.

When I was finished eating breakfast, Mom would rush me to the bathroom to make me brush my teeth. She would tell me to keep brushing until all my teeth felt squeaky and smooth when I rubbed my tongue over them.

Mom would take the bobby pins out of my hair and make bobbing ringlets with her fingers. If Mom hadn't rolled and put the pins in my hair the night before, she would tie it way up on my head in a bun or a ponytail. She'd pull my hair so tight it made my eyes looked slanted. The elastic would sometimes catch little hairs on my head and make me sneezy and itchy.

When I took the ponytails out at night, my head would hurt like I'd had my hair bent the wrong way all day. It felt so good to take them out and scratch my head.

Mom would never let me go out anywhere unless I was perfectly put together. Everything I wore had to match. Mom would even polish my shoes and boots at night so they would be clean and shiny for the next morning.

Chapter 7

CLICKING TEETH

I HAD BABY TEETH IN my mouth, and they would get loose. I loved to wiggle them and feel their sharp little tops coming away from my gums. I would wiggle my teeth with my tongue. The suction between the tooth and the hole in the gums would create a clicking sound.

My dad hated it when I played with my loose teeth when he was around. The clicking sound bugged the beegeebers out of him. Dad would chase me all around the house. He'd tell me that the tooth had to come out. He'd yell for me to come to him, and he was going to pull it out for me.

I was terrified of Dad when he was running after me for my teeth. He'd be grabbing at me, and if he caught me, he would not let me go. I made a run for it and got all the way under the double bed in their room. Dad ran in after me, and he pulled the bed away from the wall and plucked me out.

He'd make a noose out of a piece of thread and slip it around my tooth. Then he would yank the tooth right out of my head. It would hurt when Dad pulled my tooth out that way; my gums would bleed. I would much rather have played with it until it came lose, and then I could have just wiggled it out.

It was 1969 and I was seven when I went to the dentist with my mom and dad. The dentist was going to pull out all of my rotten teeth. There must have been six of them that were bad. My mom said I ate too much sugar, and that was why my mouth was full of little black teeth.

The dentist said that it would be better to be rid of the bad teeth before the new ones started growing in. The new ones would come in crooked if we didn't remove the others because they would not have had enough room to grow between the bad ones.

The nurse gave me a mask to breathe in, and I thought everything was funny after that. The dentist pulled my teeth out, and it didn't hurt a bit. I had been all scared for nothing!

When the teeth had been pulled, the dentist stuffed my mouth up with cotton. He gave me a little tin cup to take home to bleed into. I could even keep the cup afterward.

By the time I got home, everything wasn't so funny anymore. My mouth hurt. Mom gave me baby aspirin, and I cried the night away.

The little tin cup that I'd been so happy to be able to keep I never wanted to see again. It reminded me of the smell of blood and the pain that I had to endure from the dentist that day. I hated dentists after that.

Chapter 8

SUNDAYS

Mom bought Brenda and me fancy white dresses and bonnets. We wore little white gloves with the dresses. Brian had a three-piece suit with a tie. These clothes were our good clothes and only worn for church on Sunday mornings.

We would go to church every Sunday, and it was so boring. It wasn't boring for Brian because he got to be an altar boy. He would clean the priest's cup and saucer and ring the bell when he was supposed to. I didn't think he should be up there on that altar, because he was no angel.

The church had way too many rules. We'd have to kneel, stand, kneel, sit, sing, repeat things, do this, do that. I never really understood what the priest was talking about, but I knew all my cues and what to do.

There was a Sunday-school class that the kids would go to in the basement of the church after Mass. It was always fun to meet up with all the neighbourhood kids at Sunday school. It wasn't like real school at all. We would colour and make things and learn about Jesus.

They would hold tea parties in the church where they would sell crafts and baked goods. The church ladies would sell crocheted pot holders and doilies. The community would make and donate knitted finger puppets, scarves and mitts and all kinds of things for the sale.

Mom never made my dad go to church on Sunday. Dad worked hard all week, and he would often have the flu on Sunday mornings.

Mom wasn't sickly; she hardly ever got the flu. Anyway, I think she felt all of us could pray enough to save Dad too.

My dad used to drink lots of booze on Saturday nights; Mom said it was sometimes the reason for "the Sunday flu." Mom and Dad would have friends over, they would drink booze, and Dad would get drunk.

He wasn't a bad drunk or a mean drunk. He was kind of funny. The neighbours loved to come over and drink with Dad at our house because he was so good at it.

Sometimes Dad was embarrassing when he drank too much. Like the time he was eating pizza. He had a piece of pizza in his right hand, and his left hand was holding his head up while he sat at the table. He kept telling Mom he was hungry and was bugging her for more pizza. He'd forgotten he had a piece in his hand already.

It was funny until my friends saw him and started laughing. Then I was mad at him, and I was mad at my friends for laughing at him.

Chapter 9

DRUNKEN EARS AND SCARY TALES

I T WAS A DARK AND windy winter day in 1970 and we were visiting at my aunt and uncle's house, and the adults had been drinking all day. Mom and Aunty Lilly started talking about getting their ears pierced. Uncle Mel said he could pierce them. Mom wasn't sure if she was brave enough to really get them done.

I told Mom I would get mine pierced first, if she would get her ears done after me. She didn't think I would do it.

My uncle took a clean ashtray, poured some whiskey into it, and told me to keep dipping my fingers into the whiskey and rubbing it on my earlobes. I did what he told me to, and my earlobes became numb. I guessed that my ears were drunk.

My uncle put a bar of soap behind my ear. One ear at a time, he stuck a sewing needle through my earlobe with a piece of thread attached. He tied the thread into a loop. He did it so quickly I didn't feel a thing.

Mom couldn't believe I had done it, but she kept her word and sat down on the coffee table in front of Uncle Mel to get hers done next. She let Uncle Mel pierce them, and she cried and thought it was so painful. She did not rub the whiskey on her ears beforehand, so her ears were too sober, I think.

I was told to keep my earlobe holes clean with rubbing alcohol at home, but Uncle Mel didn't have any rubbing alcohol at their house to use. That's why we used the whiskey from the ashtray. I was supposed to pull the threads back and forth each time I rubbed the alcohol on them to keep the string from sticking and the holes from closing up.

The next day my ears felt like they were on fire.

I had to sleep carefully in my bed for that whole week. It even hurt to have my ears touch the pillow. Once my ears had sobered up, they were so sore.

One of the holes wouldn't heal; it had yellow stuff coming out of it. We had to take the thread out and keep the hole very clean until it closed back up.

I had to get someone to remake the hole in my ear, and Uncle Mel wasn't around. Mom took me to a neighbour lady who thought she could re-pierce it. The neighbour lady put an ice cube behind my ear. She was shaky and slow, and I couldn't bear the pain of the ice cube being there so long. I cried and begged Mom, "Please, just take me home. I don't care if I have it pierced!" Mom thanked the neighbour lady for her efforts but told her to forget it, I was too upset.

Mom and I went to a girl at the mall to have the ear re-pierced. It hurt a lot less to have the hole made the mall girl's way than the neighbour lady's way. The mall girl took my ear and then shot an earring pin right through it with a gun. It stung for a few seconds, and then she gave me another earring pin to put into the other ear so I had two to match.

The earring was bigger than the hole in my ear, and the girl had to push the pin earring through the old hole and make it bigger. I thought she should have just shot my other ear too.

My ears stayed a light pink for a short while and looked like normal ears after that. I was so happy that they healed all right this time. I was so tired of having them touched when they were hot and sore, and I thought I looked so grown up with earrings.

Every Saturday night we'd have company over, and Mom would get up early Sunday morning to get rid of the beer bottles and dirty ashtrays. She would clean the house before we woke up and got ready for church.

I thought drinking and smoking was disgusting, and I never understood why people had to put whiskey into a good drink of pop and ruin it like that.

After work, my dad would go to the King George Hotel. The King George was just a hop and a skip away from our house. If mom was in good humour, on the weekends she would join Dad at the hotel and leave me with Brian and Brenda for the evening.

Dad would go to the hotel at night after work. Mom was not happy with him being there for too long. She would get me to call the hotel and ask for Roger Marcoux. I'd have to tell the barkeep that it was Poochie Marcoux calling, and to please send Roger Marcoux home because his dinner was ready.

Dad would try to fool us sometimes and tell the barkeep to say he was not there. We knew he was, because we could see his truck outside of the hotel. Sometimes my mom would cry because she was so upset with my dad for always being at the King George.

Brian would boss me around when he babysat me. He would tell me very scary bedtime stories that would give me nightmares.

He'd always make me think he was going to be good to me and tell me a nice story to help me sleep. The tale would start off nice enough. Then in the middle of it, he would twist it into some terrible horror story. He wouldn't let me leave the light on in the hall either, and then it was dark and I was scared.

One of Brian's stories was about a guy who had golden hands. A robber came into the guy with the golden hands's house while he was sleeping and killed him. The robber cut off his golden hands and brought them home.

The robber put the golden hands in his bedroom dresser drawer to store them. He went to sleep that night, and then he woke up because he heard his drawer opening. The robber was terrified when he saw the golden hands rising from the drawer and coming toward him through the air. The golden hands grabbed the robber by the neck and strangled him to death, right there in his bed.

More often than not, Brian's bedtime stories were bad. I finally told him I didn't want to hear any of his stories anymore because I didn't trust him to be nice to me.

After arguing with Brian one day, I had to be convinced by my mother I was not "a mistake," as Brian had tried so hard to make me believe.

Mom said I was the only child in our family who was "planned." I just looked at Brian with a *ha ha ha ha ha* and said to him, "You were the one who wasn't really wanted!"

Our house was medium-sized with three bedrooms. Brian got his own room because he was the only boy. He had a record player and records and all his own stuff in his room. He told me to keep out and to never touch any of his things.

Brenda and I had to share our room, a dresser, a closet and the room's little bit of space for our things.

Brian liked to fight with me—pulling my hair, pinching me, poking me and calling me names all the time. Brian would try anything to hurt my feelings.

I would borrow things from his room when he was not around, just to spite him. When he was back home he'd ask where his things were. I'd tell him, "Oh, Mom told me I could borrow that!" It would really bug him to even imagine me being in his room.

I searched his room one time when he was out, and I never found anything good in it. I don't know why he was so protective of it.

Chapter 10

LORD OF THE THINGS

*D*AD WORKED HARD. HE ALWAYS had a physically demanding job, and the mining jobs he had were often dangerous ones. He was what they called a raise miner or a hard-rock miner, and he would often get hurt. He'd come home with all sort of pains from work.

One time, he came home in a taxi. He walked in with a limp, wearing a neck brace. A rock had fallen on him while he was drilling above his head, and it had hurt his neck and back.

Dad's hard work gave him big muscles. He was very strong.

Dad purchased a big dump truck. He always had a regular truck, but this was a huge truck with great big wheels and a dumping box. He must have talked about it with my mom, because she let him get it. Mom and Dad would both tell us that Dad was the boss, but we knew Mom was really the boss.

Dad came home with this big green dump truck, and we were so excited to go for a ride in it. Dad started it up with all its noises and black smoke. He let Brenda and Brian and me, along with some of the neighbourhood kids, stand in the big box on the back of the truck, and he took us into town.

Dad drove us to the general store. We were standing in the back of the truck, waving and yelling at everyone we saw, acting like we were a carnival act. Then Dad bought us ice-cream cones and took us all back home.

This truck, Dad said, was a way for him to make some money working for people. He would haul dirt or rocks or gravel. He would shovel stuff into the back of the truck for neighbours, to take it away for them. He would take stuff to the dump for people.

I loved it when Dad would bring me to the dump with him. There were often huge black bears walking around, and they would run away when we drove in.

Dad always told me the bears were way more afraid of us than we were of them.

There was a big old bear on the road into the dump one time when we were going there to drop off some garbage. The bear was in the way. It was directly in front of the truck, standing straight up on two legs and looking right at us. My dad honked the horn of the truck and yelled at the bear. The bear didn't move. Dad had to decide whether he was going to drive over the bear or turn around and drive away.

Mom was telling Dad, "Let's just leave!"

Dad said, "That big old bear is not going to get the best of me!"

Dad wanted us to know that he was the boss and not the bear. He was not going to just let that old bear get his way. My dad got right out of the truck, waved a stick at the bear and yelled "Shoo, shoo!"

The bear nonchalantly walked off in another direction and disappeared into the trees beside the dump. I thought to myself, *That old bear did not look more afraid of me than I was of him!* I wouldn't want to run into him in the bush all by myself.

Dad figured he was the reason the bear left. "I showed him!" Dad said gallantly, and we continued on into the dump.

Going to the dump, to me, was like being a pirate searching for hidden treasure. Dad and I would poke through all the garbage with sticks and come home with all sort of things that Mom would be disgusted with us for. We'd wash our finds up to be like new things again and agree with each other that we'd found some real bargains.

One time, Dad and Brian and I were at the dump, and Dad had found a whole pile of potato plants that were growing there. He started picking them and putting them into the truck.

Brian and I couldn't believe that Dad was really going to bring those potatoes home and expect us to eat them, right from out of the dump.

Dad brought the potatoes home and put them into our basement potato bin with all our own garden potatoes. I don't think he even told Mom about the dirty old potatoes.

We all forgot that he put those dirty potatoes in the bin. We must have eaten them and never knew any different. I guess they were safe to eat after all. Dad would always look for potato plants when we went to the dump after that.

Dad liked to have a new vehicle, or at least one that was new to him, every so often. We had an old white car for a long time, and then Dad called us to tell us he was bringing a new car home. Mom shook her head, wondering why Dad was never happy with the things that he had.

I was so excited. I couldn't wait to see what the new car was going to look like. When he drove it into the driveway, I was so angry with him because it was another white car.

We might as well have kept the old one, I thought. I walked around it and didn't think there was anything special about another white car.

I thought my dad was real smart and that we were rich. He was always buying things like boats, cars, trucks, campers and houses.

One time my mom told him, "Don't buy any more houses. I'm getting old, and I am tired of painting and cleaning houses."

Dad would move us into an old house, finish it up nice and buy another house. We'd either sell or rent the house that we were living in, and he and Mom would start all over again with another house.

We always had at least one house we were renting and another we were living in. My dad was the landlord. I felt it was important for the people living in our houses to know that my dad was their "land lord," the king of the castle. I figured the people living in our house should be grateful and look up to my dad. I told them I could kick them out any time I wanted to because my dad was the landlord.

When my dad found out about me saying that to the renters, he was very angry with me and shouted, "Poochie, we should be grateful to them, not the other way around. The renters are paying off our mortgage, and our property will get paid for only because of them."

I was humbled by him in front of the renters. From then on, I kept my mouth shut so as to keep my foot out of it.

I felt pretty silly every time I'd run into the renters for a while after that.

Chapter 11

SPAGHETTI AND CANNING

MOM WAS MAKING SPAGHETTI IN the kitchen. It was my favourite meal. This time, she had no tomato paste, but she would not tell me that until I complained at dinner that the sauce was wet and slippery and wouldn't stick to my spaghetti. I didn't like it.

My mom got angry with me and said, "You eat your spaghetti or else. There are orphans all over the world with nothing to eat. They'd be happy to have what you have!"

I never really understood how one thing had anything to do with the other. It wasn't like I could just put my spaghetti in a box and send it to them.

I'd move the stuff around on my plate while everybody else ate. When I'd finally piled it in a way I thought made it look like there was less of it, I would ask to leave the table to go to the bathroom. I'd stay in the bathroom until I heard the clinking of glasses being collected from the table and the water being poured to wash the dishes.

My family ate really fast. I imagine it all started with my dad when he was little. I figured it was probably because he grew up in a family of 11 kids and sometimes they'd have lots of food and sometimes just a little. So he'd have to eat fast to get enough to fill his belly before it was all gone.

When Dad was done eating dinner, he wanted sweets for dessert right away. My mom baked something every day. She was well-known for her peanut-butter Special K squares with milk-chocolate icing.

Dessert was brought to the kitchen table and put in front of Dad right after his last bite of supper. If you wanted dessert, you had to have it when Dad was done with his dinner. So we'd hurry up and eat so that we wouldn't miss it. Sometimes you were so full you weren't even able to get it all in you.

But if you weren't hungry when the food was on the table, you would just have to wait until the next meal. Later, if you were hungry again, maybe Mom would feel sorry enough for you to let you have a bowl of cereal or some toast and jam.

My mom and dad spent a lot of the summers and the autumns gardening and weeding and collecting vegetables. In the fall, they would spend most of the time in the kitchen making canned beets or tomatoes, carrots, and bread-and-butter pickles. My mom also made the best, saltiest dill pickles in the world. They wouldn't even last us until the following year. Neighbours would ask for some of her dill pickles.

She'd put a big pot of boiling water on the stove, and the glass jars would boil in it to sterilize them. Dad had to help because when the vegetables were in the jars, Mom needed someone strong to close the lids good and tight. Making preserves was a together kind of thing.

Mom would take all of us strawberry-, blueberry- and raspberry-picking in the fields of the old farm where she grew up. I hated picking berries in the tall fields of grass. It was so hot in the summer sun, and the bugs would be swarming around you, biting you. The branches were always picky and would leave my legs and arms all scratchy and itchy.

Mom would always bring me to pick the berries with her because I was a "clean picker," she said. My dad would come and pick, and Mom would always curse him when it came time to clean the berries. He'd have leaves and twigs and half the bushes in the pail with his pickings.

We'd go around to fruit farms and pick apples, pears or peaches, and Mom would make apple pies or canned pears and canned peaches that were yummy too.

I loved Mom's peanut-butter cookies. She would put little fork prints on the top of them to squish them down before she put them into the oven.

Mom made butter tarts, and they were the best in the world. No raisins or nuts or anything. Just drippy, gooey brown-sugar filling and flaky pastry. They were so sweet your cheeks would hurt when you ate them. I could never get enough of them. I thought, *Them orphans that want my spaghetti are never going to get my butter tarts, they'll have to fight me for them.*

Chapter 12

FIRE FRIES

MOM WOULD MAKE FRENCH FRIES in oil that she'd boil in a pot on the stove. There were never enough french fries for me. I could hardly wait for them to get cooked. I'd be jumping up and down asking her to take them out of the oil so I could eat them.

Mom took them out early once because of my begging. She thought that I wouldn't eat them because they were still white. I ate them, all white and oily; I didn't care how cooked they were. Mom said it was gross to eat them like that, but Dad and I liked even raw potatoes with salt for a treat.

Potatoes were good no matter what—unless they were mashed. I didn't like mashed potatoes because they were mushy, like somebody had already eaten them and spit them out. If I found a lump in them, I would gag. Mom would take a few boiled potatoes out of the pot for me before she'd mash them.

I had a friend named Donna. Her family was making french fries one night in a pot on the stove, the same as Mom and I did. The grease jumped out of the pan, and the kitchen started on fire. The whole town stood on the road in front of Donna's house that night and watched her house burn down.

I don't think I had ever seen the Nairn fire truck outside of the Nairn firehouse before. It was the most exciting thing to ever take place in our town. The firemen tried to get the fire under control, but they couldn't. Donna's whole house started caving into the fire, and it burned right down to the ground.

The next morning, everyone in town went back over to see what was left. It was a smouldering pile of black ashes, and nothing was left that you could recognize. It smelled like a fire that had been rained on. It was an awful sight.

I couldn't imagine losing all of our family treasures like our photographs and Mom and Grandma's handmade quilts. Having everything we own just taken away like that forever. Never to see any of it again. But Donna and her family were happy to have gotten out of the house alive, and that was good enough for them. They didn't seem to be too bothered by the missing memorabilia at all.

Maybe they didn't have valuable homemade things like we did. They thought they could just replace all their stuff with store-purchased things and hand-me-downs. They had to fill their new house up buying and collecting things, one piece at a time. There were no more mementos or souvenirs from their past. Nothing for them to look back on and remember.

I would visit Donna in her new house. There was a strange feeling of emptiness in the new place. It felt like something terribly important was missing.

I thought it would be devastating to have that happen to me. From then on, I was going to make it a point to know where everything important was in my house, in case I had to run around saving things from a fire.

Chapter 13

HANGING TEX STAR

EVERY EVENING AFTER DINNER BRIAN and Brenda had to do the dinner dishes. Brian would sing, and he wouldn't stop singing until Brenda got mad. You could hear him in the kitchen, his voice getting louder and louder.

Brenda would yell to Mom, "Please make him stop!"

My mom would say, as always, "Brian, that's enough. Do I have to send you to your room?"

Brian was always getting yelled at. I think he liked it. He spent a lot of time in his room whether he wanted to or not.

One time, when he was in Grade 8, Brian was doing a project for school. He was working on an electric chair that was going to kill Tex Star, a rubber cowboy doll he used to play with when he was younger. His project was all about the ways to execute a man.

The electric chair consisted of a tin bottle cap that would fit on Tex's head. It had a wire soldered onto it, and it was connected, somehow, to the chair and to a nine-volt battery. Brian had little pieces of duct tape cut to look like restraints. The little restraints were taping Tex Star into the chair by his hands and feet.

If you touched the bottle cap when the wire was connected to the battery, it would make a tingling feeling on the end of your finger. Brian said that with enough time, you could smell the rubber on Tex's head burning. I never smelled it, and it never really did much to Tex Star, I thought.

Brian also made a gallows with 13 steps up to the noose and the hanging spot for Tex Star. On the stage where Tex would have to stand to get hung, there was even a little trapdoor in the floor with a hinge. The door would drop open when the rope was let go, and Tex's feet would hit the floor. There would be Tex, hanging through the hole in the floor. He'd have a little black bag wrapped around his head to spare the poor cowboy the aggravation of having to watch what was about to happen to him.

Lucky for Tex, the guillotine Brian built didn't have a heavy or sharp enough blade to cut off his little head. You would drop the dull piece of steel down on Tex's neck by pulling a string while Tex was lying there. He'd have his little head fitting right into the carved-out board that Brian had whittled out with his pocket knife. That rubber doll would just bounce under the weight of the steel blade when it was dropped.

I thought Tex had a tough life and Brian was demented.

This was the first school project I'd ever seen Brian get so interested in. He never usually had homework, yet he always got high marks in school.

Mom would brag and say Brian was very smart. "Near to genius," is what she'd say about him to people.

I heard a saying that "being a genius is just hairs away from being crazy." I figured the word suited Brian just fine then.

Brenda was smart too, but she had to work harder to get good marks. I later found this to be true for me too.

Brenda was pretty, and she always had a boyfriend. They were always boys like Brian too. I couldn't understand it. They would be mean, sarcastic, bossy boys. "What's nice about them?" I'd ask her.

Brenda was in high school when I started public school. We were pretty far apart in age—nine years to be exact.

Brian was six years older, in Grade 7 when I started Grade 1. There was no kindergarten back then. My birthday was in December, and I started school directly into Grade 1 before I even turned six. My mother thought that was a mistake because I struggled so hard to get decent marks.

Brian never bugged me much at school. For the most part, he wouldn't even let anybody know I was his sister. He didn't talk to me at recess time or at lunch hour, and he and his friends would just ignore me.

Brian was pretty popular in town. Most of the girls at school wanted to know all about him and what he was like to live with and all kinds of stupid things like that. He wasn't a bully to anyone else but me, so no one believed what I told them anyway.

Brian was a leader among his friends. I would refer to him and his friends as the badass kids in town. For some reason, he had a large following of bad kids who looked up to him. I never understood why they liked Brian so much; maybe it was because he was the only kid in town to grow marijuana in the bushes. The other kids had no idea where it was. Maybe they had to be nice to get him to sell it or share it with them.

Maybe it was because he was handsome, like the girls said, but I never believed that.

The other kids did like him, and for what reason, I never really knew—probably a good thing for him. If I'd known, I may have told Mom.

Chapter 14

HOMESICK AND ACCUSED

MOST OF THE PEOPLE WHO lived in Nairn Centre seemed to be related to me in one way or another. But I had friends in town who were not my cousins as well.

Angie was a close neighbour. Her mom and dad had stood as bridesmaid and best man in my mom and dad's wedding party. We called them Aunty Noella and Uncle Bob. I used to spend lots of time over at their house playing.

Mom and Dad and I were over visiting, and Aunty Noella asked me if I'd like to sleep over with Angie. It would be the first time I'd ever slept over anywhere. I was a little apprehensive, and my mom was hesitant but said it would be okay.

Angie and I played all day together. At the end of the day, Mom and Dad said good-bye, kissed me and left. I watched them walk to our home about 200 yards away.

I felt a big lump in my throat and started feeling anxiety. Luckily, it passed when I went back to playing and forgot about Mom and Dad leaving.

Aunty Noella made spaghetti whenever I was over; they were Italian. She would always have different shapes of pasta, bowties, shells and tubes. My mom only had the long skinny noodles. I could never convince Mom to change our noodles to something more fun.

Nighttime came, and Aunty Noella put me into bed beside Angie. I laid there while Angie fell asleep. I was thinking about my mom, how she must be missing me and what she must be doing right now.

I started to cry that my belly hurt, and Aunty Noella called my mom. Mom came over, bundled me up and took me home. She didn't seem too surprised at all.

"No more sleepovers for you!" she said. I guess she was lonesome and happy to see me back.

On occasion Mom would give me a quarter to walk to the general store with my friends One day, there were grab bags on sale for a nickel a piece on a big table at the front of the store. They were clearing out all the old candy in the store to make room for some new stuff.

I bought five grab bags with my quarter. They were filled with penny candies and little toys—balls and jacks and marbles and stuff.

I came into the house with my arms full of grab bags. My mother saw me and accused me of having stolen them. "You had to have stolen them, Poochie. I didn't give you that much money," she yelled.

"I didn't steal them!" I cried. Mom must have been having a bad day to even imagine that I would steal.

Mom did not believe me. She took me back to the store. She had me by the ear, and I had all of my grab bags to return to the storekeeper and apologize.

She walked me back into the store, in a huff, calling for the store manager. She was pretty sorry when she spotted the table full of grab bags with a "five cents each" sign over them.

Mom explained to the store owner that she had thought I must have stolen the grab bags because I only had a quarter and brought home so many things.

The store owner laughed and said, "Well, we'll certainly never worry about Poochie taking anything from our store from now on, will we?"

Mom told all of her friends about making me return the grab bags to the store. I made sure that they knew that she had made a big mistake accusing me of being a thief. If the truth didn't get told—and it wouldn't be the first time—the whole town might get everything all turned around and think I was a robber.

I thought this should teach Mom a lesson.

Chapter 15

FEELING GOOD WITH SHERRY

IN 1968 WHEN I WAS still in Grade 2, I had a friend named Sherry. She had strawberry-blonde hair and a whole face-full of freckles. She was kind of bossy and very mature for her age.

I remember running home from Sherry's place to mine and back again after school. We went to her place because her mother didn't keep a very clean house, and we didn't have to worry about making a mess of it. We didn't even have to clean it up when we were finished playing.

It was a lot more comfortable than my house. My mother was just too picky about being neat and having everything in its place. She didn't like to have to clean up again at the end of the day after she'd already done all the housework.

Mom really hated it when Dad would clip his toenails over the coffee table and not pick them up. She hated it if I used my eraser on drawings and then brushed the shavings onto the floor. She didn't like crumbs or lint on the floor, fingerprints on the patio doors or handprints on the walls.

I followed Sherry and joyfully took in everything she had to teach me. She even taught me how to make myself feel really good by crossing my legs together and squeezing. Little did I know that what we were doing was masturbating and having orgasms.

That is, until one day when I was doing the squeezing game in the living room while lying in the big armchair watching TV. My mom and Brenda were in the kitchen doing something at the table and saw me.

"Poochie!" my mom yelled, scaring me half to death. "What the heck are you doing?"

I turned red, sat still and never answered her because I couldn't really explain it. There was no real word for what I was doing. No word that I had learned.

I never did the squeezing thing in front of anyone again after that. I knew it was bad. I don't know how I knew, or why it was bad, but my mom's surprised and upset voice told me everything.

All I knew was that this great feeling I could achieve all by myself—by simply squeezing my thighs together and then letting go and repeating this action over and over until this magic feeling happened—was a no-no.

Before my mother implied to me that this exercise was wrong, I'd even done it in school once. All the kids had our heads down in class, waiting for the teacher to return to the classroom. I was bored with waiting and no one was looking. I couldn't have cared less if they were—I figured everybody must do it when they get bored.

I never related the squeezing thing to sex until later on in my teenage years. Then I learned what it was that I had been doing. From then on, I knew that any good feeling that happened like that was called sex, and it was wrong to be doing it.

Chapter 16

STAR DAZED

SHERRY TOOK TAP-DANCING LESSONS ONCE a week from a teacher of dance in the nearby city called Espanola. After she'd been taking lessons for about six weeks, Sherry started to teach me.

I always wondered why Sherry was taking lessons for tap dancing. I found I could already do it better than she could. She gave me one of her lessons, containing all she had been taught over the past six weeks, and I caught on in a blink.

I thought that Sherry should be teaching the class, and she liked that. I would look forward to learning more from her each time we got together. It was fun to pretend we were big stars and dance together for a pretend audience.

The Grade 2 classes were going to hold a concert. Everyone who wanted to go onstage could take part in presenting plays and jokes and skits to entertain our families. This was going to be a chance to get on the stage in the big auditorium that I'd watched the older kids perform on at the Christmas concert and Easter assembly.

The teacher asked for volunteers. I raised my hand, and with Sherry and me in my mind, I said, "We know how to tap dance!"

I had hoped Sherry would be my partner.

But Sherry said she had not taken enough lessons, and she just was not ready to take her tapping to the stage yet. So she would not dare to go up there with me.

The teacher said, "All right, Beverly, if you'd like, we will make you a solo dance act in our show."

I looked at Sherry and decided to go on without her, and oh my God, I was so excited.

Sherry was really upset with me. She thought I was being a phoney and a traitor.

I thought it would be fun for both of us to shine for a crowd, like we'd pretended to do at her house. When she didn't have the guts, I thought, *With all I know about tap dancing, I'd be crazy to give up this chance to be a star.*

I figured I knew how to tap dance, and I could even make up some steps of my own to make it better.

Sherry didn't pay any attention to me at school or after school anymore. She ignored me all the time. We didn't hang around together, and she didn't give me any more dance lessons. So I put Sherry out of my mind.

I thought I would keep my dancing a secret from my mom until the day of the production. I would dance for her and surprise her. She would be so proud of me when she found out about my secret talent—which she didn't even know I had! The weeks went by slowly until there was one day left before my big dance debut at the school concert. I was getting a little nervous.

The teacher asked Sherry if she would lend the school her tap shoes for the show, since I didn't own a pair.

She did lend them for me to use. I was really surprised.

Sherry cried at the thought of even going up on the stage. I think that the tap-dance school people must have told her she was not very good. She brought in her tap shoes and handed them to the teacher, who handed them to me. I took them into my hands and treated them as though they were Cinderella's glass slippers.

The shoes fit me perfectly.

I wanted Sherry to know that I would take extra special care of her shoes, because I knew how much they meant to her and her future. She would need them if she was going to get better and become a professional tap dancer too.

I taped bells and ribbons to the shoes to make them my own. I would practice and practice in the mirror until I figured I must look really swell.

The song my teacher chose for me to dance to was the very popular "I've Got Rings on My Fingers and Bells on My Toes." It was a new song by Teresa Brewer. The teacher would play the music on the record player behind the stage where no one could see her, and I would dance in front of the curtains.

The day came for the concert, and it was going to be in our classroom. The whole class helped to build a stage and hang curtains from the ceiling; we drew and painted all kinds of pictures to decorate the walls. All of the class thought it looked beautiful.

A big introduction was made for each of us by our teacher, and then one act began, and then another. You could hear the parents laughing at the jokes and clapping. And then, suddenly, it was my turn.

The teacher announced, "Here to tap dance for us today is Poochie Marcoux!"

When the music began, I sped onto the stage in an incredible whirlwind, flapping my feet and clacking my fancily decorated tapping shoes on the wooden stage floor with the music. I kept a big smile on my face and made it look like I knew perfectly well how to tap dance.

I spotted my mom in the audience—who, as I began dancing, had her mouth hanging open in awe. She slowly raised her hands to cover her mouth. I'm sure the shade of red that Mom had turned was because she was so very proud of me.

My song ended, and the people in the audience stood and clapped. I got a standing ovation. I was a star!

When it was all over, I stripped the shoes of the taped-on bows and bells and respectfully handed them back to Sherry. She very kindly told me that I had done a real swell job of remembering what she had taught me. "But some of those steps were not even real tap-dance steps," she added.

I ran to my mother's arms to get her kisses and hugs and to hear what she thought. I thought she must be so proud of me.

She hugged me and said, "Oh my, you were very impressive. Quite a surprise."

A mother of one of the kids in my class had been sitting beside my mother and asked her, "How long has Poochie been taking tap lessons?"

My mother's mouth dropped open again, and she just looked into my eyes, smiled and hugged me without giving the lady a second chance to try to get the answer.

Mom scooped me up, and instead of staying for coffee and cake with all the other moms, she took me home to celebrate and tell Dad and Brenda and Brian all about the show.

From then on, I danced in the living room in front of my mom and dad.

I'd dance every time I heard the Don Messer show on TV, with all the fiddlers. When the music finished and I'd curtsy, Mom and Dad would smile back and forth to one another and clap with enthusiasm.

Sherry dropped out of tap-dancing after the Grade 2 concert. I guess she decided she didn't want to go pro. I wondered if maybe she realized she didn't have what it took.

Sherry didn't want to be my friend anymore, but there were other kids who I could play with. There were kids who lived within walking or biking distance of the school and my house. There were plenty of other friends and cousins around to take Sherry's place if she didn't want me.

Sometimes the teacher didn't give me a spot in the stage events. I'd make myself one by becoming the music conductor who would start the other children singing with my words of encouragement—"a one and a two and a three" and I would begin the song for them to join in. I had a knack of just taking over. It amused the teacher; I figured it was in a good way.

Sudbury had a small television station with one local channel. There was a show that was broadcast right from Sudbury once a week called *Captain Cook*. It was a half-hour show hosted by a man known as Captain Cook to all of us kids.

Captain Cook would have a classroom of kids from a different school in the Sudbury area on TV with him every week. The children from the chosen school's classroom would sit on bleachers that were set up in the studio. Captain Cook would ask questions and talk to the kids about their schools and where they lived. At some point during the Captain Cook show, they would have a couple of people performing a dance, a song or a skit.

Nairn Public School was chosen to appear on the Captain Cook show. The classroom that was chosen to go was mine. The teacher started looking around the class for children who could perform either songs or skits on the show.

I was so hopeful that I would catch her eye and she would pick me, and she did. When she asked me to do something on the show, I figured she would probably want me to dance. My lucky stars must have been shining that day, because I was the first kid chosen.

But I wasn't going to dance this time. I was going to sing.

Wow, I thought, *I didn't know I had that talent either.* But the teacher was the teacher, and she must know if I could sing or not, and she chose me. Therefore, I would be proud and happy to do that.

For weeks before our classroom's turn came to go on TV, the whole class would go over the answers to the questions we knew Captain Cook would be asking us.

We all rehearsed our parts. We were so excited to be going on TV. I was going to sing a song called "Clean Face." Captain Cook would call out for Poochie Marcoux, and then he would help me out from the bleachers and walk me up to the microphone to sing my song.

However, when it all happened and the microphone was put to my mouth, I was so frightened that I forgot the words to the song. Thank goodness the teacher helped me out by singing it with me, and I was happy to have gotten through it without crying.

My mom and dad and everyone in Nairn watched it, and I was the talk of the town for a while.

However good I might have been, though, singing was not my forte. I would rather have been Captain Cook!

Chapter 17

CHRISTMAS

MOM WOULD START BAKING AROUND the middle of November. By the time Christmas came, there were mountains of sweets and goodies in the house—peanut-butter balls and chocolate coconut rolls, squares of all sorts, and my favourite, Christmas shortbread cookies with cherries on the top.

She would make what we'd call "shit on a stick" out of pork with a batter of seasonings that she cooked in the oven on a stick, like a kabob. Everyone loved them. Mom or Dad would ask us, "How much do you love me?"

We'd answer, "More than shit on a stick!"

Brian and I would watch all the Saturday morning cartoons. Around Christmas, they had so many commercials marketing new toys. We would ask for whatever was new, one thing after another. Our lists got bigger and bigger.

Mom would take our lists and mail them to Santa. I couldn't understand why Santa never wrote me back or why he never got me half the things on my list. I imagined you must have to be perfect to get everything on the list that you asked for. I wasn't that willing to change my ways.

Mom always had a few gifts for us from her and Dad. She would put them under the tree early. I would shake them and try to guess what they were. But Brenda and Brian never seemed too interested in the newly placed gifts. I never could understand why it didn't excite them as much as it did me.

Mom and Dad spent a lot of time visiting and shopping around Christmas time. The King George Hotel would have "Hockey Night in Canada" on TV, and that drew in the townspeople and my parents.

There were also neighbours and extended family getting together and sharing the Christmas cheer. Brian and Brenda would be "stuck babysitting me," as they would say, whenever Mom and Dad went out.

On the weekends, when Brian and Brenda babysat me, they would put me to bed at the same early time as my weekday bedtime, but they would get to stay up. They sat in the living room drinking pop and eating chips without me, watching their favourite TV shows.

I was under their watch near Christmas when I woke up to a strange noise in the living room. All of the lights in the house were off except for the colourful ones on the Christmas tree. I got out of bed and snuck into the living room, where I'd heard the noise coming from. That noise turned out to be the sound of unwrapping gifts.

I saw Brenda and Brian sitting beside the Christmas tree with all of their gifts from Mom and Dad opened in front of them.

"What are you doing?" I yelled.

Brian jumped and screamed, "What are you doing out of bed? You little vulture. Vulture!" he yelled. "Damn you!"

Brenda sat me down on the couch beside her to talk to me.

Brian started taping the wrapping back onto his bunch of gifts.

"We were just sneaking a peak," Brenda explained. "We'll let you open one of yours, if you won't tell."

Brian looked over at me like I was the devil herself.

"Okay," I said. "I won't tell."

"You think you can trust her?" Brian said with a sarcastic tone.

"What choice do we have?" answered Brenda.

"We could kill her," Brian joked.

"You can trust me, just let me open one up too," I pleaded.

They let me pick out one of the presents that was labelled to me. Brian sat and watched while Brenda helped me carefully open the present of my choice, so we could put the tape back on it the way that it was. That way Mom would not know that the gifts had been tampered with.

When I got the package opened, I was so disappointed. I had chosen a gift box with panties in it. Panties with the days of the week sewn on them. *Aw, not fair,* I thought.

Brenda helped me tape it all back up, telling me to remember that I'd promised I would not tell.

Brian told me to raise my hand and make a pinkie swear to promise a vow of silence. I did the pinkie swear, and then Brenda brought me back to bed and tucked me in.

I wished they were Santa's gifts under the tree that I could have chosen from. He wouldn't have given me panties for Christmas!

I never did tell Mom and Dad, because I had been an accessory to the crime.

Chapter 18

SCROOGE

O N CHRISTMAS EVE, WHEN I was ten, on the way to my dad's sister Aunty Fern's house, Brian ruined Christmas for me. Dad had the car started and all of us were in it and waiting to go. Dad and Mom said they had to go back into the house to get something they had forgotten.

Brian whispered, "There is no Santa Claus, you know, Poochie!"

I just turned away and tried to ignore him.

"Why do you think it takes so long for us to get out of the driveway every Christmas Eve? It's because Mom and Dad have to go back in and put the presents under the tree for when we get home. That way it appears as if Santa Claus came while we were away," he explained.

When Mom and Dad returned, I asked them if what I'd heard from Brian was true. Mom turned around in her seat with disappointment in her eyes and said, "You had to tell her now, Brian?"

"So it's true?" I cried

"Yes, I suppose you're old enough to know now," Mom admitted to me, right before we left to go to Aunty Fern's.

I was so upset. I felt betrayed by everyone in my family. I was so angry with smug old Brian especially. Finding out that there was no Santa Claus on Christmas Eve sucked. I felt that knowing the truth was going to ruin this Christmas and probably every Christmas to come.

"I hate Brian!" I shouted out loud.

Dad just put the car in drive, and we drove away like nothing had changed. My family said nothing else to me all the way there. They just expected Christmas to carry on as always.

Christmas had lost its magic forever. I'd had a pretty good idea that Santa was not real anymore, but hearing it just made it much less possible to create the magic in my head.

Chapter 19

THE CANVAS SHACK

IN 1968, WHEN I WAS five, my father purchased a camp on Lake Agnew, west of our house in Nairn. It was located on the same dirt road that my mother's family farm had been on when she was a child. It was about 10 minutes farther into the bush, beside a lake. There was about an acre of land with the camp on it, and it cost Dad five hundred dollars.

The camp was built out of four timbers posted into the dirt. There was a huge canvas tarp wrapped and stapled around the posts. A window was somehow constructed into the front of the camp, and there was a door frame with a door on the side.

We used a little outhouse to go to the bathroom. We pumped water from a pump with a handle that came up from the ground in the middle of nowhere.

The pump was fun. We could pump and play in the water as much as we wanted to. Dad never gave us heck because he said this well was never going to run dry, not unless the lake was empty.

We had a lantern Dad would light every night after he pumped it up with coal oil. There was an old pink woodstove in the corner that kept us warm on the cold days when we were there.

After Mom had cleaned and oiled the woodstove, she would slice potatoes really thinly. We would all throw the sliced potatoes right on the hot stovetop. They would get a little burnt, but with butter and salt, they were a very delicious treat.

A heavy iron sat on the woodstove. You had to attach a wooden handle to it to lift it when it was hot. You could use it to get wrinkles out of clothes, but it would leave rust marks on them.

There was a toaster rack made of wire. You would stand the bread up on it to toast. The toast always got burnt on the rack, and I hated burnt toast.

We had a portable cupboard for our food and dishes. A sink sat on the countertop by the front window. A pipe went straight outside through a hole made in the canvas wall. It emptied all of the water right onto the ground outside of the shack.

We had to bring water into the camp from the pump outside. We carried it in buckets to use in the sink, for doing the dishes.

We'd bathe in the lake, and we had to use Ivory soap to wash with. It was the only soap that would float in the lake. Other bars of soap that didn't float would sink to the bottom and get sand on them. Scrubbing your skin with them was like using sandpaper.

There was no washing machine at the camp. Sometimes we'd stay for a long time, and Mom would wash our clothes in the lake, on a washboard, and hang them on a clothesline to dry.

The floor of the camp was made of big boards with big cracks between them. You could see chipmunks popping their heads up through the knotholes.

When we woke up in the morning, it was either really hot or really cold in the camp. We could look into the sunlight coming through the front window. We would see all the dust particles suspended in midair in the morning haze.

We had big canvas sleeping bags on our beds that had cold canvas on one side and itchy, scratchy, picky wool on the other.

Brenda and Brian and I begged for flannel sheets to use as a barrier between us and the picky wool sleeping bags. Otherwise, it almost hurt to go to bed.

The roof of the camp was made of tin, and when it rained, it was loud inside. My mom always loved the sound of the rain beating on the roof.

We usually ate our meals at the picnic table Dad had built. We had the picnic table placed in front of the camp so that you could watch the lake and the sunsets while you ate.

I loved the atmosphere in the old camp, the smell and the feeling that existed there. We had no electricity and no TV; there was just my family and me.

The beach was a bay full of weeds and driftwood, and the bottom was made of sand. Dad decided we would have a beautiful beach if we cleaned it up.

We and the neighbours who would later use the beach to swim worked really hard to clean it up. We pulled out stumps and logs and weeds, and raked the shores of leaves and twigs and other debris. The men from the camps in our bay used their boats to drag large logs and stumps to empty bays and drop them there to rest.

It was a beautiful beach when it was cleaned up. It had yellowish-white sand and clear, clean water. Dad and the neighbour men built a dock out of trees. They put a long black rubber mat down on the dock to keep us from getting slivers when we walked barefoot. However, the black rubber would get so hot from the sun that you'd have to run when you were on it or it would burn your feet. The rubber was very slippery when it was wet too.

I would beg Dad to build me a campfire every night. When he got tired of always having to make the fires for me, he taught me how to make them by myself. I became a real firebug, and I lit fires every night for all the kids and everyone else to enjoy.

I loved poking the hot red coals with a stick. I'd burn wieners and marshmallows and throw the occasional toad in the flames.

If it was raining, Mom and Brenda and Brian and I would stay in the camp and play Steal the Pack, Crazy Eights and Monopoly, which my brother had to win or he pouted. Brian would borrow money and buy everything that he landed on. He would have a whole stretch of places that you couldn't get by without landing on one. Then you'd have to pay him an enormous amount of rent.

Once he accomplished buying up half the board and repaying his borrowed money, it wasn't long until he'd have houses and hotels everywhere. Brenda and Mom and I would run out of money paying him the fees and rent to land on his properties, and he would win.

He was a poor winner, Mom said, and an even poorer loser. He would get up and walk like a chicken, cluck and laugh when he won. He'd try to make Mom and Brenda and me feel dumb. When he lost, he would get angry, make a fuss and throw things.

I had to sleep with Brenda in the big bed in the living room. Brian got the cot under the window in the living room. He had Band-Aids on the holes in the canvas to keep the bugs from coming in and biting him and to keep the raindrops out.

Sometimes Brenda was nice to me, and she would cuddle me to sleep. Sometimes she ignored me. I often wondered what she was thinking about when she didn't want me near her. I think sometimes she only cuddled me because she was cold.

I always thought she had picky, hairy legs. I hated the scratchy feeling of them when they touched my legs in our bed. When I was mad at her, I would call her Gentle Bren, after the bear Gentle Ben I'd seen on a TV show. Brenda's picky legs made me want to have my own bed.

Aunty Noella and Uncle Bob, who lived beside us in Nairn, moved into the camp next door. The surrounding property had three old original shacks built on it. We bought our shack first. Then Uncle Bob and Aunty Noella and another couple from Nairn bought one. My mom's sister, Marie, and brother-in-law, Raymond, bought some property right next door, and they built their own camp.

We named our bay Booze Bay because there was always lots of booze being drunk in it.

Uncle Bob and Aunty Noella had five kids: David, Tina, Donald, Angie and "Puppy" (that's what everyone called the littlest girl). When they were at the camp, Angie and I played together. She and I were close in age.

Aunty Noella would get mad when Angie and I didn't want to play with Puppy. Sometimes we'd be nice to her, and sometimes we would not. Puppy got in the way, we thought. She was too much of a baby for us. I acted pesky and mean to Puppy, just like Brian did to me.

There was a boy who had a camp around the bend from us, and his name was Michael. I played with him on occasion, and we would say we were boyfriend and girlfriend. One time Michael was walking toward our camp, and I was looking at him, studying him. He was smaller than me and skinny and kind of scrawny, I thought.

Looking at him, I said to my mom, "I don't know why I love him so much, I think he's kind of ugly."

Mom laughed and said I was silly talking about love at my age, and that beauty was in the eye of the beholder.

Later on in my youth I had a crush on Donald, Angie's second-oldest brother. He was tall, dark and handsome, I thought. When I'd see him at school, after camping on weekends together, I'd blush when he would talk to me. I tried to hide it, but it became obvious. I know he knew I liked him, because it was not very long after that he took me to the rink shack behind the schoolyard to be alone with me. We would sneak behind the rink shack and draw long lines or short lines in the sand. The lines were to indicate what kind of kiss we were going to give each other. We'd give a long kiss for a long line or a short kiss for a short line.

I thought the sneakiness of kissing Donald was fun.

We did the kissing game often. He was my boyfriend, I thought, until one time I had to go out of town. When I returned, Donald had started going to the rink shack with another girl, in a higher grade, and he didn't want me anymore. I was very hurt by him, and he didn't even notice.

I cried for days. I couldn't believe Donald did not like me the way I liked him. How could I have been such a fool?

Mom could not figure out what was going on with me crying all the time. I did not tell her about Donald because she'd already told me, with Michael, that I was too young to be in love. I didn't want Brian to know either; he would tease me and embarrass me, probably in front of Donald.

My family would go to the camp every weekend. When it was warm enough to swim and bathe in the lake, we'd stay for weeks in the summer without going home in between.

We went to the camp early in the spring when there was still ice on the lake. I'd beg Mom and Dad to let me go in swimming. Mom said, "Go ahead." She thought that I wouldn't get past my toes.

I jumped off the dock, right into the water, and then swam right back out. The water was so cold it would hurt my toes when I was in it. But I was always happy to be able to say I was the first one in the lake that year.

I loved swimming, and I had it down pat by the time I was six years old. My mom would get upset with me whenever I was in the water. She couldn't swim, and I'd go out too far for her to come and get me if I needed saving.

It was neat being able to do something that my mother couldn't do. I spent lots of time in water over Mom's head, showing her that it was just that easy.

When Brenda and Brian were young, they had gone to the river in Nairn with Mom and Dad, and they were swimming with a big inner tube from a tractor. They went out too deep, and Brian let go of the tube.

When Brian realized that he was over his head, panic set in. Brenda, who could hardly swim herself, swam out to save him. Brenda was over her head, and the two of them started using each other to push up on to get out of the water.

They bobbed up and down trying to get away from one another, and they both started drowning.

Mom saw them and was screaming, "Rog, Rog, Rog!" She was helpless. She had to find Dad to get him to swim out to save them.

I guess that was why Mom was so afraid to let me go into the water on my own. She was always uptight when I'd tell her I wanted to go swimming. She didn't want me to go over her head unless Dad was around.

But I did go way out in the lake by myself, and Mom grew more trusting in me and my confidence in swimming.

Chapter 20

THE PRO FISHER

MOM AND DAD BOUGHT A nice big wooden boat. We kept it tied to the dock at camp. We'd go fishing in it in the evenings after dinner.

I hated fishing . . . until I caught my first fish in the summer of 1971, when I was 10 years old.

Mom and Dad and I were out in the boat, on the lake. I was playing in the water and got a bite and was sure I felt it. Dad said, "Give it a yank to set the hook!" I yanked it, and I caught it good. It was a big fish, too!

I was terrified when the fish started pulling and undoing the line on my reel. It was really hard to keep reeling the fish in. My arms started to hurt, and I was getting more and more afraid of what I might be pulling up. I asked Dad to please take my rod and finish bringing in the fish for me.

"Nope, it's your first fish, and you've got to bring him up yourself!" Dad replied.

I was scared, and I started crying. When I saw the fish, though, the tears stopped, and I started to get really excited.

I pulled in a beautiful five-pound pickerel. My dad got the fishing net, caught the fish with it and pulled the fish into the boat when it was close enough.

Dad held my large catch up in front of me. He got the scale and the measuring stick. He weighed and measured my fish. Dad said, "This is no doubt the biggest fish we've ever caught in our lake!" He was proud of me.

I was so excited. I just wanted to get my fish back to the camp to show the others what I'd caught.

Dad bragged about me and my fishing abilities after that. I was a real fisherman from then on. Every time we went out to fish, I would get lucky and catch anywhere from four to eight fish, every single time. Often, no one else in the boat would even get a bite. Nobody could understand how I kept catching fish when they were not even feeling bites.

It amazed Mom and Dad, but I'd just come to expect to catch fish every time we went out. I had a knack for feeling anything that touched my line from under the water. I'd reel them in, and the fish would be hooked through the fin or the tail. I'd haul them in one after the other. Everyone who fished with us would stand there, mouth hanging open, as I kept reeling fish in.

I could sense when something was touching my line or if I was touching something that was stationary. I would give the line a jerk and haul up whatever it was that was down there.

I started taking out the old canoe that my brother had bought and abandoned. I would gear it up and go fishing by myself. I'd catch minnows from the dock in a minnow trap that Dad taught me how to set. Dad taught me to put bread in it to attract the minnows, tie it to a branch and leave it to fill up.

Dad and I would drive up to the old farm where my mom grew up. We'd walk through the deep weeds to the swamp to get minnows. Dad said, "There are always more minnows in the swamps than in the lake."

I was always terrified of running into a snake in the long grass at the farm. I knew there had to be lots of them in the wet rushes.

Dad and I would set the minnow trap and come back later on, or the next day, to check it. The trap would be full of dark little swimming things. Dad would stick his hand right in and get rid of the bloodsuckers and the pollywogs.

We'd put the minnows in a pail and bring them home for fishing. I picked the big ones out for me to fish with. I thought the bigger the minnow, the bigger the fish it would bring in.

I didn't mind touching the minnows, but even Dad didn't like the leeches. Later I found out he was afraid of snakes too.

I would bring minnows, worms and rubber gloves with me to go fishing. I wouldn't touch worms; they gave me the heebie-jeebies. The rubber gloves were to put the worms on or take the fish off the hook. I wouldn't touch the fish either. I also didn't eat fish.

I'd have my minnows in the bait bucket and the canoe pushed off the shore, and I was ready to go. My mom would yell, "Poochie, you won't catch any fish in the middle of the afternoon sun."

I'd pay her no mind and set out on my way.

I'd have to paddle like crazy and bring a bailing bucket because the canoe had a leak in it. I would find a spot where I imagined there would be lots of fish, put my toe into the hole in the bottom of the canoe to stop the leak, and start fishing and reeling them in. Usually I'd just catch some little bass or perch, or the odd pike. On occasion, I'd catch another nice pickerel and bring it home to my mom and dad.

I caught a ling one time and it looked like a flat black snake. Lucky for me, I had my handy-dandy little pocket knife in my tackle box, because that fish was just hideous. There was no way I was going to touch a ling, even with the rubber gloves on.

I cut my losses and snipped the line to let him go. I let the ling swim away with my hook, line and sinker. It gave me the shivers to think that I swam in the same water that the ling was living in.

We had lots of sinkers. Dad would melt down lead he would find at the dump and make containers of them. He would pour the lead into a mould that he'd made himself. When the lead had cooled, we would take the sinkers out of the moulds and use them on our fishing lines. Dad was so handy like that.

Dad and Mom only went fishing in the early mornings or in the evenings. They claimed that the fish did not bite in the daytime, only the morning and evening.

I knew that was what Mom and Dad believed, but I never believed any such thing. The same rules did not apply to me. Plus, I hated getting up early in the morning, and I didn't like coming home in the boat in the dark with the mosquitoes biting and swarming all around my head.

Chapter 21

MOM'S GUEST

*A*UNTY FERN WAS MY DAD'S younger sister. Her family brought their camper and stayed on our property next to our camp for the summer vacations starting in 1969 when I was seven.

Aunty Fern always said what she thought, no matter what it was. Sometimes she would be harsh and right to the point with things. Sensitive people would get hurt, and other people just took her words and used them as constructive criticism. I appreciated her honesty and her bluntness.

Aunty Fern's husband, Alphonse, was almost 15 years older than her. They had seven kids together: Paulette, Yvette, Rita, Gerry, Colette, Claudette and Dianne.

They all spoke French when they spoke to each other, and they taught me some French.

I'd sit in their trailer with them and play a French card game called Mille Bornes. It was a card game in which you had to get to 1000 miles to win. Everyone picked up cards throughout the game and put down cards like flat tires and out of gas cards that prevented the next player from moving on until the repairs were done.

I learned the names of all the French cards. I'd say the names, and it made everyone laugh to hear how I would pronounce them.

Colette was one year younger and Claudette was one year older than me. We really got along well. We'd sleep outside in their big kitchen tent in our sleeping bags.

I remember Colette waking up with a giant green icky caterpillar in her sleeping bag one morning. It was the biggest caterpillar we'd ever seen.

Collette was terrified of bugs, spiders, flies and especially caterpillars. She jumped up and down; she shivered over and over thinking that the caterpillar must have touched her, since it had been inside the sleeping bag with her all night.

Collette's frightened antics made Claudette and me laugh so hard, we almost peed our pants. We were just lucky that it wasn't one of us that the caterpillar decided to terrorize, because we'd have freaked out too.

Poor Colette wouldn't sleep in the tent again with us after that incident.

The three of us would lie in their camper in the warm summer afternoons when our parents would go out to town. We would read scary magazines with murder stories. We would get each other so afraid with the stories that we couldn't leave the camper to go to the outhouse without holding one another's hand to get there, even in broad daylight.

We went skinny dipping when it got dark. Just the girls went into the water to swim naked first. We had done something silly that made my Aunty Fern laugh, and her false teeth had fallen out of her mouth. We had to search and search for them in the dark water. We were all cold and ready to stop swimming, and we still hadn't found the teeth.

We had all kinds of theories about where they might be. We thought a crab was probably walking around with them on, or a big-mouthed bass might be wearing them. We laughed, but Aunty Fern was afraid she'd never see them again. I guess she would have had a heck of a time eating without them.

The boys went swimming after us, and they were going to search for the teeth while they were in the water. Brian found the teeth right beside a crayfish. "He was trying to put them on," he laughed.

When school ended in the summer, Mom, Dad, Brian, Brenda and I would go to the camp for the vacation. Mom figured I was bored when I was alone, and she'd get tired of entertaining me and having me following her around. She decided to take it upon herself to invite a friend to the camp for me for the week.

Imagine my surprise when Mom came back from town with Sherry. I was angry. Sherry and I had not been friends for a long time, and I didn't want anything to do with her.

Sherry walked into the camp and looked at me playing on the floor with my Barbie dolls. I just looked back up at her with a big frown.

She had a smug look on her face like the cat that swallowed the canary. Sherry knew I would be upset to have her brought up there by my mother without my having asked her to come. But she thought it would be funny to humiliate me, I guess.

My mom smiled at me and said, "Look who I brought for you to play with."

Sherry came and sat down beside me. She picked up one of my Barbies. I just looked at her and then back at my mom. I stood up, grabbed all my Barbies—including the one in Sherry's hand—and stomped past her and Mom to go outside, yelling angrily to my mother before the door closed, "You brought her up here. You play with her!"

Sherry stayed, and Mom played with her for about a day and a half. Finally, I caved in; I started to feel sorry for Dad, who couldn't have been real happy not having anyone to play with himself now that Mom was so busy trying to occupy Sherry.

So I befriended Sherry once again to save Dad from loneliness.

I learned a lot about Sherry. She had become one of the badass kids in Nairn since we parted. Sherry told me things that she and the badass kids would do together. I showed her things that I did at my camp in the summer when I was all by myself.

We canoed together, made sandcastles, swam and had huge bonfires. It was just like old times. We seemed to be becoming good friends again. We never talked about the tap dancing episode.

I enjoyed sharing all of my experiences with Sherry. She was quite impressed by all the things I knew about camping and fishing.

When summer was over, Sherry left the badass kids behind a couple of times. She joined me for some good clean fun, but her curiosity in the badass's direction ended up getting the better of her, and she went back to hang out with them. Sherry and I remained friends, but we didn't see each other much.

I tried to hang around with the badasses once, with Sherry. They were crude—swearing and smoking and talking nasty about everybody.

I tried to figure out what it was that the bad kids thought was so bad about their lives. I asked them, "Why do you feel that you have to resort to disobeying the adults and always doing forbidden things?"

All of them had been ignored or mistreated by their parents. They felt that they were not worthy of anything or cared for by anyone. These badass kids felt that they were out to pay the world back for all of its unkindness.

I guessed they would rather have people look at them and think they were bad than not look at them at all.

I asked them, "Why don't you just shut your ears to the bad stuff people say? You don't have to let them bother you, you can just ignore them and take care of yourselves!" They would just call me Miss Goody Two-shoes and tell me I was a spoiled brat.

They looked at life like they were doomed and hopeless. I just didn't ever feel that way about life. So we kind of butted heads and never could relate very well to one another.

Chapter 22

UNCLE RAY

WE LIVED IN A HOUSE right beside my Aunt Marie and Uncle Raymond's house. Uncle Ray also bought a camp beside ours in Booze Bay. They never had indoor plumbing or running water at either of their places. In their house in Nairn, they had a pump that always had cold water coming out of it.

They used to have a big, portable, round steel tub in their kitchen that hung behind the wood stove. It looked like a big cauldron. The big tub was what they used to bath in. When they had a bath, they would have to warm the water in a kettle on the woodstove and pour it into the big tub.

I always pictured my big, fat Uncle Ray sitting in that steel cauldron in the middle of the kitchen floor, the woodstove raging nearby to keep him warm and a candle beside him so that he could see. He had a big round belly and a big red nose. I envisioned him bathing in the tub and looking like he was in a Norman Rockwell painting.

Uncle Ray and Aunty Marie did have electricity, but they didn't have a lot of money, so they had to be very thrifty. They had a black-and-white TV. I remember sitting on the carpet on the wooden floor with one of Grandma's knitted afghan blankets watching *The Ed Sullivan Show* with them on occasion.

My uncle Ray loved his little old house. Whenever he was not in it, he would be outside in his outhouse, reading the newspaper.

Uncle Ray and Aunty Marie had two boys, Wayne and Dennis, and a girl, Connie. They were all closer to Brenda's and Brian's age.

Connie got her own room, which was really a closet. There was just enough space for a bed, and if she grew any taller, she'd have to start sleeping bent in half.

The boys slept in bunks in another room slightly bigger than Connie's room. Uncle Ray and Aunty Marie had a little bit bigger room. In it was a big lumpy feather bed that you almost had to walk sideways to get around. The kitchen and living room were one room.

Their house had wooden floors. I never imagined you had to sweep or clean the floors, because they were black and everything would just get swept into the cracks anyway. Their house had probably been the same way when pioneers lived in it back in the 1800s.

I loved the atmosphere in their little house and spent lots of time over there. Aunty Marie did try to keep it clean, but it never really looked any different when it was clean than when it was dirty.

One night my brother, Brian, was sleepwalking. He went over to Uncle Ray and Aunty Marie's doorstep in the middle of the night. He was there all night, sitting on the stoop. When Mom and Dad got up to get Dad off to work, they panicked. No one knew where Brian went.

It was about five a.m., and Dad found Brian on Aunty Marie's front step with his fishing rod in his hand. Brian was waiting because "Uncle Ray promised to take me fishing, and I want to be ready!" he said, still asleep. Dad picked him up, brought him home and put him back to bed without a fuss.

The next morning when we were all awake, we talked to Brian about being over at Uncle Ray's and waiting. He didn't remember a thing.

Brian used to sleepwalk a lot. He'd have big glassy eyes, and he'd yell at my mom and dad. You knew he had to be sleepwalking because he would never raise his voice to them normally. Dad would have slapped him on the head, the way Dad always did when he was mad at us, with his big fat index finger.

I never sleepwalked, but I did something one cold wintry day that could have made me look just as foolish. I remember touching my tongue to an aluminum screen door we had at our house to see if my tongue would really stick to it, like people said it would. Turned out that it was true, and there I was with my tongue stuck on the door.

I got scared that I would have to get my tongue cut off to get free. I tried to yell for help, but I could hardly get any noise out. I had put so much of my tongue on the door that it was stretched out as long as it could go. Mom was in the house, I had the screen door half opened and half closed, and I couldn't move.

Luckily, with some prying, it became loose and I got free.

I was relieved that it got unstuck before Brian got home from school. He would have made a laughingstock out of me.

From then on, I swore I would keep my mouth shut and my tongue to myself.

Chapter 23

COUSINS

MY CLOSEST COUSINS, DEBBIE AND Linda, lived in the house directly behind us. Their father was my dad's younger brother Harvey.

Harvey's eldest daughter, Debbie, was very tall. I think she must have come out that way as a baby. From as far back as I can remember, I had to look way up at her. Linda was my size, but in high school she sprouted up way past me too.

Debbie would like to find dead animals and things, touch them, and poke them with sticks and stuff. I thought she was demented or evil sometimes. She could be mean to me and to Linda, and we never knew why.

One day my mom came around a corner when Debbie was just about to hit me over the head, from behind, with a block of wood. Another time, Debbie hit Linda over the head with a rake. Linda and I were afraid of Debbie. I did like her when she wasn't moody. Linda was usually happy and always likeable.

Debbie and Linda both had long, straight bodies. I had a short body and a big butt.

I said to their mother, Aunty Evelyn, "I don't know why I had to be so short with such a big butt. I would like to be straight and skinny like Debbie and Linda. They look like athletes." Debbie and Linda giggled.

Aunty Evelyn said, "You laugh, my girls, but in the future you will both wish you had Poochie's figure."

Aunty Evelyn always made me feel good about myself. She pointed out my differences as being special. I liked Aunty Evelyn. I always felt that she really liked me too.

Debbie and Linda and I spent time together colouring and listening to music, usually Elton John records. We would sit and sing the songs over and over to learn all the words by heart. We would play dolls, and Debbie would always have life-sized dolls that her parents would buy her.

Uncle Harvey and Aunty Evelyn lived right behind us, and they were digging a well so that we could stop having to share our water. We were tired of running out of water.

Uncle Harvey had huge cement culverts delivered to their house to put into the ground for the well. They had them stacked two on the bottom and one on top. The other was alone in their backyard. Debbie and Linda and I used to play in them and pretend that they were individual apartments.

Our parents put a stop to us playing in the crocks because they started to roll a little bit and had become dangerous to play in.

One day, Debbie, Linda and I went to the dump with my dad. He was on his way there anyway, and he asked if anyone wanted to go along for the ride. We all wanted to go. We got there and begged Dad to let us stay for half an hour just to look around. Dad didn't mind. He liked scavenging too, so he went off looking for potatoes and stuff.

Debbie and I found a whole garbage bag full of baby clothes. We brought the bag home, and Aunty Evelyn washed all the clothes. They fit Debbie's big doll perfectly.

I thought Debbie was so lucky. My mom always bought me little dolls like Thumbelina or Baby Go That Away. They were dolls that were so small, they were more like kittens than babies. I asked Mom, "Why can't I get a big life-sized doll like Debbie's?"

Mom replied, "Because you're just a little girl. Your babies would just be smaller. Debbie is big, and she would have bigger babies!"

Obviously, Mom didn't understand that playing mommies just didn't feel real when I had to have a baby the size of a pop bottle.

I didn't get any of the baby clothes from the dump, but my mother would knit my little babies all kinds of outfits out of wool and Fentex. On occasion, Mom and I would go shopping, and she would buy my baby a new outfit at the department store in Espanola.

I had cousins spread all over the north and south of Ontario. It was mostly the ones in the north that my family would visit. My father had many of his siblings living in nearby towns and cities. We would spend most of our time with Aunty Fern's family on the weekends.

One day Aunty Fern called us and, with distress in her voice, asked us to please come over because Claudette had cut off her thumb and Aunty Fern didn't know what to do for her.

They told us that she had the thumb in a box, and they didn't know what to do with it. Mom told them to put it on ice, and we hurried into our car and left for their house.

We hurried into Espanola to see them. Cousin Claudette came to us with a little box with her thumb in it, all bloody. My mom and dad looked at her thumb in the box, and while they were looking, Claudette wiggled it and scared the heck out of them. She had put her thumb through a hole in the bottom of the box, covered it with cotton batten and poured ketchup all over it to make it look real, like it was really cut off.

We had a good laugh over that practical joke. Aunty Fern said that they just wanted to get us to come to their house for a visit.

I never understood how come all of Aunty Fern's daughters had such big boobs and I never had any. Mom told me I was maturing slower, which was normal for some kids. She said, "Boobs will come soon enough!"

They never did come. Even my period didn't start until I was 14.

Most of my girlfriends thought that maybe I was not normal, because it seemed like I was never going to get my period. Most of them had been menstruating since they were 10 or 12 years old.

My cousin Debbie told me not to wish for my period, because my whole life would change after it started. I would be a woman, and there'd be so much more expected from me. I resolved to stop thinking about it; I decided to hope that it never came.

The Marcouxs would have family reunions each year with as many as 500 people showing up sometimes. I felt like I was popular there. With a name like Poochie, I suppose I was pretty popular anywhere. Not too many people forget your name when it's strange.

When a relative from far or near would drive onto the reunion site, all of the family would gather around to greet the newcomers. It was wonderful to have so many people treat you as family. We were a big, close family—half the size of the world, I thought.

There was one cousin, Henry, who nobody really liked because he was an old drunken beggar. Our reunion site was held in a gravel pit once, and Henry told us kids to put up his tent for him. Henry got very drunk, as usual, and when bedtime came, he was stumbling around looking for his tent. We all laughed and pointed him to it, on the top of the gravel pit where we had pitched it for him earlier that day.

He waddled up through all the gravel, got into the tent and slept there. We never thought he really would be able to stay up there, balanced on top of the gravel pile, but he did.

It was funny in the morning when Henry woke up and unzipped his tent. He found himself way up on the hill over the rest of the reunion-goers. He looked dumbfounded and couldn't figure out how he'd gotten up there.

Henry just rolled down the hill, got up, walked to the big tent and got another beer, ready to start another drunken day all over again.

The Marcoux clan would rent a large piece of farm property or a field somewhere. We would put up a lean-to with lights and electricity for a stage and a dance floor. When evening came, the musicians would play for us.

We had a band of musicians that played music from the south of Ontario and another band that would play music from the north. They would compete with each other to try to be the most entertaining. The music was fantastic. We'd dance until the musicians were exhausted.

We, the little Marcouxs, always tried to stay up all night long—trying to pull an all nighter, we'd call it.

This family weekend was one of the few times that our parents knew that we, the children, were all safe and looked after by everyone. They didn't have to worry about us. We tried hard to stay awake and usually couldn't make it all the way until morning.

For dinner, we would have a huge cauldron that we'd boil corn on the cob in. There was enough for us all to eat as much as our hearts desired. One of the uncles would bring it from his family farm.

I'd fill my belly up with corn, dance all night long and run around with all of the other kids. I'd fall asleep by the campfire when all the excitement died down. There were always relatives still awake in the early morning hours, sitting up visiting with family they hadn't seen in a while, drinking and talking by the fire. They would make sure we woke up and went to bed with our mom and dads, in our campers, before the sun came up. I'd get into my camper where Mom and Dad would already have been asleep for hours. I'd crawl into bed quietly so nobody knew that I was even there. But Mom always knew what time I came in. I think she waited up for me sometimes.

Some kids would be playing with the bongos all night long. Bongos were an annoying instrument when just banged away on all night, without any skill or rhythm. Everyone would wake up and complain about the noise that went on all night. The next night, the bongos would get taken away and hidden from the kids.

We had horseshoe tournaments and darts tournaments with real trophies that had been kept in the family for years. The darts competitions would sometimes get very intense.

We'd have three-legged races and potato-sack races for the families and kids. We'd have raffles with things that people would make. Everyone would make things throughout the year for this special event.

There were hand-carved furnishings, knitted blankets, wooden plaques with clocks on them, rag dolls and jewelry to raffle. There was even homemade moonshine that Uncle Carlos had made especially for the raffle. Everything was handmade.

We would all buy tickets and put them in the jar in front of whatever we wanted a chance to win. On the last day, there would be a draw. The proceeds would go to the Marcoux treasurer, who would put it toward next year's rental site and celebration supplies.

We had a jail that some of the older men had constructed. We would hold kangaroo courts in the big tent. The convicts were people accused of swearing too much or drinking too much. Usually it was the older members like Henry who were accused and arrested.

They would have to plead guilty and pay a fine or stay in jail until they could prove they were innocent or reformed. It wasn't really that strict of a jail. It usually ended up with everyone, including the arrested person, laughing outrageously at the accusations made.

Like the raffle proceeds, the money the Marcoux family made from the jailhouse went toward the following year's reunion.

Chapter 24

HEADQUARTERS

ONE YEAR WE HAD OUR reunion at a place called Headquarters. It was a campground just off of the Spanish River, near where the scow to get to Nairn from the other side of the river went back and forth. When my mom and dad were children, they would take the scow across the river from my mom's parents' farm to go to school or work in Nairn.

You could drive your car up onto the floating wooden scow and pull it by hand. A cable kept it in place and is what you would use to pull you and your car across. You'd go right across the river to the bank in Nairn and drive off again.

Apparently, my mother's walk to school was "six miles long and uphill both ways," as my dad would say. Mom went to school in Nairn in a two-room schoolhouse with one room for Grade 1–4 and the other room for Grade 5–8. Mom got as far as Grade 9 because in her last year of public school, there was a new teacher who came to town to teach that grade. So mom got to stay another year.

Dad had moved with his family to Nairn from Kirkland Lake. He and his family were putting in sidewalks for the city. Dad had started school and got to Grade 2. Then my dad's help was needed at home. He would miss so much school to do work that he finally quit school and worked steadily with his family. Dad's parents felt it was more important that my dad help at home than waste his time in school.

Dad went out and got a paying job when he was still at a very young age. He got his driver's license shortly after starting to work.

To get his license, all he had to do was show the ministry that he knew how to drive the car—no test or written exam.

My dad bought his family's first truck with his money from working. Dad's parents had him turn the truck over to them for the entire family to use. They did not have a lot of money, so whatever anyone in the family got had to be shared by all.

Dad said his mom used to make big Sunday dinners, and she'd be in the house baking all day. She would have to make seven pies just to feed the family dessert.

My dad's family would go fishing. Before he met my mom, Dad told me, he had once been out in a boat with his dad when they lived in Quebec and reeled up a dead body from the lake. The body was all green and bloated. Apparently this body was a former worker from the mill. Dad said it was the body of a man who everyone heard had gone missing a few weeks earlier.

Dad said no one around was surprised or upset to find this man dead in the river. It sounded like maybe someone had just done him in and nobody cared, by the way my dad talked. I thought it was pretty weird. Dad just thought that the body was pretty scary when they pulled it up fishing. He said it was something he will never forget. *I guess not!* I thought to myself!

My mom used to babysit for Dad's two younger siblings. Dad and the rest of his family would go fishing for their dinner. My dad used to walk my mom home afterward, and that was how they got to know each other.

My father asked her to go to the show with him one night as he walked her home from a day of babysitting. She accepted his request, and at thirteen, my mother fell in love with my father, who was eighteen. Three years later they were married. My sister, Brenda, came along shortly after. Once married, Mom and Dad never did anything apart. They were like conjoined twins.

Years later, when we had our family reunion at Headquarters, we had to fix and clean the old abandoned house that stood on the property. It would be restored for all of our older-generation Marcouxs to stay in while they were at the reunion. Many of the old people were not able to sleep outside in tents and trailers because they had back problems or arthritis or they were just too old. They could not bear the cold or they could not get up from the ground in a sleeping bag or cot, so we would make them decent accommodations wherever we camped.

While we were fixing up the old house for our family reunion, a cousin, Peter, was being a ham. He was performing for all of his female cousins, including me. We were sitting up in the loft all lying across the beds watching him. Peter was flirting and joking and acting silly.

The door to the loft was a hatch in the floor. The door was opened and leaning against the wall behind it, so the floor had a big cut-out hole with stairs going down from it. It was easy to overlook if you weren't paying attention.

While Peter was playing around in the dimly lit loft, he forgot that the hatch was open and walked directly over the hole. It was almost like a cartoon where the character stays there for a moment and then realizes where he is and falls.

When he did fall, he went head first and passed out when his head hit the bottom. We were all amazed at how quickly it happened. We were terribly worried about Peter. One by one, we ran down the stairs after him. Our parents all came in when they heard the bang of Peter's head hitting the floor.

We had to take turns watching him for the evening to make sure he wouldn't throw up or pass out or die. He seemed to be all right, but we weren't sure if he'd gotten a concussion from the fall. We didn't want to let him to go to sleep in case he never woke up.

Peter recovered all right, and that year's reunion was a hit. We would remind him of his crazy antics that night at all the future reunions.

On more than one occasion, we held the family reunion at our camp. But the family kept growing and growing until our property just wasn't big enough to hold everyone.

When we'd have the reunion at our camp, all of the neighbours would be invited to come and join us. Dad said it was only courteous to invite them. This way, they would be a part of the noise and commotion that would go on all night long and not get upset with us.

The neighbours loved our family reunions and talked about enjoying it with us for years after. They were happy and honoured to be a part of our huge celebration of family. Usually friends and neighbours were not allowed to come.

My mother's brothers and sisters were spread out all over the north of Ontario. My mom's closest baby brother, Homer, and his wife, Rosy, lived down by the river in a very old one-room house with their son, Pat, and daughter, Shelly.

They had a kitchen and sitting area on one side and a curtain up in the center of the house for the privacy of their bedrooms on the other side. They had an outhouse that was outdoors, and their house also had a hand pump for water.

Pat used to sit in the desk behind me at school and pinch my butt between his shoe and my desk chair. Then he'd laugh and tell me, "You'd better come to play at my house after school, or I'll beat you up!"

I hated Pat. Besides his mean, bossy temper, he peed the bed at night. I thought he was disgusting and a nuisance. Shelly, his little sister, was just as annoying. Shelly was a little female version of Pat. They liked to get really rowdy and fight and hurt one another.

My grandmother and Aunt Margaret lived at the end of our street. My Aunt Ann and Uncle Norm lived in McKerrow, a little town to the west and just off the road on the way to Espanola.

Mom had only four siblings with the same last name as hers: Peter, George, Ed and Margaret. Aunty Marie and Uncle Felix were from Grandma's husband before she married my mom's dad. Homer and Ann, her younger siblings, were from grandma's latest past husband, Elmer. They were the closest to Mom, because Mom often had to look after them.

My Aunty Marie's husband, Raymond, died of a heart attack when I was just young enough to remember. Uncle Raymond was big and fat, and he was very kind and friendly. He had taught me to swim after he and Aunty Marie built their camp next to ours. I was very little, but I still remember the big palm of his hand against my belly as he held me over the water and told me that he was going to let me go, and I should keep on kicking.

Uncle Ray's dying really threw me for a loop. I didn't understand death. It happened so fast. I went to the funeral because it was at my Aunty Marie's house next door. Back then, the living room was called a parlour, and folks always laid out their dead family members in it when they passed. In a ladies' magazine a long while back, it was announced that the parlor should not be used for displaying the dead. It should be used for the living, and that was how it got the name the living room.

Viewings for the dead at home were becoming less and less popular when I was a kid. Only the people who could not afford to rent a place to put their deceased would still have the wakes at their homes.

My mom told me that when her dad died, she was five years old, and she remembers having her dad lying dead in his casket in the parlor for three days. She was afraid to go into the parlor because she didn't want to see him there. It caused her fear, anguish and grief to have to go about regular daily business with a dead man in the house, even if it was her own father.

I was curious to go to a funeral, so my mom took me. It was the first funeral I had ever been to. The casket was open, and Uncle Ray lay in it. He looked like a plastic doll.

I wanted to touch his hand just to see what he felt like, all dead like that. My mother told me I could touch him. I was a little afraid that he would come back to life and grab me. But I went forward and touched him anyway. His hands were cold and smooth and felt waxy. I poked him a couple times.

"You see," she said, "he's not in that old body anymore, he's gone to heaven!"

I kept thinking, as I watched his face, that he was going to smile at any time and say, "Surprise, just kidding, I'm still alive." But he stayed there like that all day. I stared at him, all of the time I was there, in disbelief.

After a church service was held, the casket with Uncle Ray in it was carried to a hole in the ground where they were going to bury him. They were just going to drop him and that box down, down into the ground. Bury him up with dirt and forget about him. I was so disturbed by this whole concept that I didn't want to leave him. It bothered me immensely to think that someday this would happen to my mom or dad.

What if Uncle Ray was just sleeping? How could we do this to him? What would Uncle Ray think of us just throwing him away like that?

I was traumatized by the idea of death after that. I remember waking up at night, crying uncontrollably, as I imagined it happening to my mother or father.

Mom would comfort me and tell me, "Don't think about it if it causes you so much grief." It was easy for her to say, but it was hard for me to do. To just keep something out of my head seemed impossible. I could not imagine my life going on without her or dad.

Trying not to think about something was harder than trying to think of it. I tried constantly to keep myself distracted from the thought of death. It did come and go every now and again, and it still bothers me now when I let it come into my mind.

I could never decide if I wanted to be buried in a hole with dirt thrown on me, unable to get out, or if I'd rather be put into a big oven and cooked to death.

If I was buried, there would be bugs and worms crawling all over me in the ground, and my body would rot and turn into a skeleton. On the other hand, what if getting cremated meant no afterlife because you destroyed your body? Maybe you needed your body planted to be able to grow again and come back. Like a seed grows in the ground, when it is nurtured by the sun and the rain. I was very confused about which route I should take when it was my turn.

Mom would say she wanted to be cremated, and she did not want to have a wake or a funeral. "I don't want anybody looking at me when I am dead," she'd say.

I got mad at her and pleaded with her to allow me to see her after she passed away, just to make sure she was really dead and to say good-bye. She would say, "Only my kids then, but just pop me in the oven immediately afterward, before I start to stink."

Nightmares would start happening again every time we talked about death, and they would stay around for weeks to haunt me.

Within five years of Uncle Ray's passing, my Aunty Marie "died of a broken heart," the rumours around town said. It was because she was so lonely without Uncle Ray around anymore.

I prayed I would die with Mom and Dad, or I would hopefully die first.

These bouts with death felt so close to me. Death was so traumatic that the entire idea of it became an obsession for me. I loved my parents so much; I often wondered how I had been so blessed to have them for my own. I prayed to God to please not ever take them away from me.

I don't know when I finally stopped thinking about it, but I was glad when the dreams and thoughts of death stopped reoccurring in my mind.

I supposed Mom and Dad had their share of hard times living with the aunts and uncles who raised some of my crazy cousins. I couldn't imagine having a whole houseful of kids like Pat or Shelley or even Brian for that matter.

When Brian and Brenda were not around, my mother would give me chores to do. I would ask, "Why always me?" I thought she had been pretty lucky to have grown up with all the kids in her family. There would have been so much help to clean her house.

I would tell her, "When I grow up, I am going to have a child for every chore so that just one kid won't have to do everything."

Mom would just laugh and say, "Yes, Poochie, you're just so hard done by!"

Chapter 25

THE WRATH OF PAT

I WAS IN GRADE 3 and I had became quite a chatterbox in school. I got the strap from my teacher, Mrs. Hayward. She couldn't get me to be quiet and pay attention. She had warned me three times before she got the strap out of her desk, walked up to me, made me put my hands out palms up and gave it to me. Whack, whack, whack.

A neighbour, Carol, who I was talking with also got the strap that day. We were instructed to put our heads down on our arms, which were crossed on our desks, and think about why we were being punished. The strap didn't really hurt much, but being humiliated in front of the whole class did.

Carol and I sat with our heads down and kept looking over at each other and giggling to try to make it less embarrassing for each other.

My cousin Pat was in a particularly bad mood that day and told me if I didn't come to his house after school he would tell my dad that I had got the strap at school. My father had already advised Brenda, Brian and me that if we were ever to get the strap at school, we would get it worse at home. So I was really afraid of this happening to me now. I wondered how hard Dad would hit me.

I told Pat I would go with him to his house after I asked my parents if I could. I begged him not to tell them about the strap. He agreed.

He followed one step behind me all the way home. My dad was standing on the dirt floor in the basement of our house, sawing wood to build new stairs up to the front door. As we ran into the house, Dad turned off the electric saw.

"Uncle Roger, Uncle Roger, Poochie got the strap at school today," tattled Pat as quickly as he could get it out of his mouth.

Eek, that damn Pat! I thought.

"Is that the truth?" my dad asked.

I stood motionless, afraid of answering him. Pat smiled and said, "Yep, ask anybody in our class!"

"Go upstairs," my father yelled to me. "I'll deal with you later. Pat, you go home," he said. "Poochie's not allowed to go out and play today."

As I walked upstairs and passed the kitchen window, I saw Pat walking out of the driveway, even madder at me now because he had to go home and play by himself.

He looked up and saw me and hit his hand with his fist. "You'll pay for this," he said, in silent gestures. And I knew what that meant.

The wrath of Pat would be worse than the belt of Dad. I would have to run like heck home every day after school to avoid Pat, now and forever.

It seemed like an awful long time, upstairs, waiting for Dad to come up and wallop me. He kept me agonizing and fearful right until dinnertime.

I was sitting down at the kitchen table when Dad came in to eat, and I waited to be scolded. We sat together for dinner every night. I just knew what the conversation would be about tonight.

After discussing my whole school strap occurrence with Mom and Dad, I explained that Carol also had a part in it and had gotten the strap too. I didn't want them to think I was alone in this.

I told Mom and Dad that now, because they did not let me go to Pat's after school, Pat was going to beat me up. I would have to run from him forever, and my life was a mess.

When they heard that Pat had threatened me, they didn't quite think I needed the belt too, I guess. I was just put to bed early, and I was told to think about what I had done wrong and not let it happen again.

I overheard Mom and Dad talking about whether to believe me about Pat or not. I guess they decided that Pat and I would deal with it on our own, or maybe they thought I deserved it.

Maybe they thought I could fight Pat and win. I didn't think I would win. I pictured myself with my eyes black and my face bleeding, limping and struggling to get to my house after being beaten nearly to death by my own cousin.

I could hardly sleep that night. I did not look forward to going back to school.

The next day, Pat got into the classroom before me. He made sure that everyone knew what had supposedly happened to me after he left my house after school the day before, or so he thought.

The other kids thought I was pretty tough because I got the strap at school and then again at home. I didn't really want to talk about it.

I wanted Pat to get distracted before the end of the day and forget about his threats. But Pat reminded me more than once during the day that I was going to "get it" later. The whole day seemed to be going by so quickly.

My cousin Debbie wanted to know all the details about the whole strap thing, like it was some kind of morbid trauma that had happened and she'd missed out on seeing it. She hung out with me at recess, and we got really involved in a conversation about bullies. Debbie thought that Pat was a bully.

Debbie told me that nobody liked him, because of his bullying. She thought that it was time someone taught Pat a lesson. "He's not so tough," she said. "I'll show him!"

Debbie liked me, and she wanted to help me. We plotted an alternative to my being beaten up by Pat.

Debbie wanted to fight Pat for me. She was ecstatic about it. She couldn't wait to beat him up and show him who's who. I couldn't believe my luck. My fear finally started to ease, and I felt a great sense of relief.

When the bell rang and we all started to walk home, Pat ran up behind me and reached out to pull on my jacket to stop me. I froze on the spot.

I was shaking and scared that Debbie might renege on the whole plan.

Debbie was right in front of me, and she made sure that Pat saw her stop. Debbie rolled up her sleeves and gave Pat a look that would scare anyone.

Debbie dropped her books and started briskly walking toward Pat. I can't even describe the terror that Pat had on his face. Pat knew that Debbie was going to do him in, and he started to run. Debbie was way taller than him and much more intimidating because of all the dead things she liked to poke and play with.

"You better run, Pat Badgerow, and don't you ever try to bully anybody again, because I'll kill you!" she yelled as Pat booted down the road as fast as his feet could take him.

All of the kids walking beside me laughed and pointed at Pat as he ran home screaming, "Somebody, help, help, Debbie is going to beat me up!"

From then on, Pat was no longer the school or the town bully. Nobody was afraid of him anymore. Debbie didn't ever have to threaten him again. He was pretty humble at school from then on, and Debbie, whom I thought was the greatest, was now my best friend.

Brian had even heard about the fight. He poked fun and belittled Pat. As for Pat, even the badasses that he used to think he fit in with didn't want him around.

The more time I spent with Debbie, the more I realized that she was not so very evil or demented, just curious.

She said, "I wasn't really going to hit you on the head with the block of wood that day, and the rake hitting Linda's head was an accident. Linda walked into it on her own and blamed me because I laughed at her."

Debbie was very convincing, and I had much more to gain by being her friend than not. So I decided to take her word for it, and we became best friends.

I never feared anyone in town again, and people started being a lot more respectful to me and my pal Deb. She never did try to kill me.

Chapter 26

THE LIVING ROOM

DEBBIE AND I WOULD SPEND lots of time at my place because her mom, Aunty Evelyn, was even pickier about how clean their house was than my mom.

Uncle Harvey and Aunty Evelyn had a humongous living room with bright orange-red shag carpet and walls painted royal blue. There was a tiny blue couch, an armchair and a TV in the room, and that was all. We kids never sat in their living room because they did not want to get it dirty. We always sat at the kitchen counter, or we played in Debbie's or Linda's room. So strange, I always thought, so big and empty and unused—their living room was like being in the community center.

At my house, you could live in and play in the living room. You just had to clean up after yourself, or you would never get a second chance to play in it. I knew the rules. I understood that my mom worked hard to keep it nice and she expected us to do the same. I knew what she wanted done because I would help my mom on cleaning day. I would help her with the dusting and vacuuming and laundry.

One time we had had lots and lots of company over for dinner. When we all finished eating, I got up on my own and started clearing the table for Mom. When the dishes were all done and the people had left, Mom gave me a quarter and said she was so proud of me for just taking the initiative and doing it on my own.

The quarter was nice, but hearing her say that meant a lot to me. From then on, I tried to help her out whenever I could.

Mom would go out some days to visit friends or drive to Espanola for an appointment. I loved to surprise her and have all her chores done for her by the time she came home. She would be so happy. Mom would tell people that I was such a great helper, and she didn't even have to ask me to help her.

Dad was always working at the end of the school day, but Mom was there when I got home from school. In the evenings, I would sit on the arm of her rocking chair while she did the *Sudbury Star* newspaper's crossword puzzle, every night. Everybody knew you had to be really smart to be able to do the *Sudbury Star* crossword puzzle.

I had a lot of respect for my mom and her education. I knew she was very smart.

When I got a little older, my mom got a job as a counter helper and a gas-pump server at Pomfreys Texaco service station in Nairn. I was upset that she would not be there when I got home from school anymore. On occasion, she would be away working for the whole day. Sometimes Dad and I had to warm up dinner that Mom would have already cooked for us, wrapped up and put in the fridge.

When Dad got home from working at the mill or the mines, he was exhausted. Dad would lie on the couch and tell me which channel he wanted to watch. I would get up and put it on for him. I would sit at the coffee table drawing.

Someone told me once that you can telepathically communicate with someone by closing your eyes and imagining a large blackboard. Imagine picking up the chalk and writing down whatever you want to have on the blackboard. Then take the blackboard in your mind and continuously spin it around as you think of who you want to send the message to.

I did this telepathy thing with Mom one night when she was at work. I wrote "Hickory Sticks" on the blackboard. I spun it around and forgot about it.

Later on, when Mom came home, she had bought me—you guessed it—a bag of Hickory Sticks.

I was stunned and told her what I did. She just said, "I knew you would like them." I tried to do it again and again with different items, but it never did work out the way it did that first time. I guessed you only got one chance, and I'd used up mine on Hickory Sticks. What a waste of a good wish.

In Nairn, there were three television channels and no converters. One of the channels was French, so really we only watched two. It seemed like there was never very much to watch besides hockey and baseball.

The French channel looked good, but I could never understand it. My parents were both French, but my mother never really spoke the language after her father died and my grandmother married her third husband, Elmer, who could only speak English. Mom was only five at the time, so she lost most of her French.

My dad would speak to Mom in French when they were debating whether or not they wanted to take a trip to the store to get an ice-cream cone, or if Dad was contemplating going fishing without me. Dad would only say things in French to her because he didn't want me to know what he was saying.

In school, I had to take French classes, and then I did know what he was saying. From then on, the jig was up! I'll never forget the surprised look on Dad's face the first time he talked to Mom about going to get an ice-cream cone in French and I agreed, "I would like an ice-cream cone too."

He just laughed and said, "I guess you know too much French for me to get away with that anymore!"

Mom liked working at the service station. She also liked the spending money it gave her. She felt like she was a real working woman with her own money.

I think it kind of scared my dad that my mom was becoming so independent. Dad didn't want her working on the weekends, so she only worked during the week. When Mom didn't work evenings, she was home to have dinner with us.

Dad was happy when he felt like he had control of Mom. I understood, from that, that men expected to have control of their wives. From Mom's reaction, I learned that it was better to just let the man think that he had control, to keep the peace.

Occasionally at dinner Dad would let us turn the TV toward the kitchen table to watch his favourite TV shows. His favourite shows were *Bonanza* and *Batman*. Brenda and Brian and I liked them too—everyone except for Mom.

Mom would get angry and say, "Do we have to have that friggin' idiot box on all the time?" She hated the TV becoming a part of our dinner ritual. She was afraid that the TV would take over someday.

Mom didn't like that we didn't chat. We were all too busy watching and listening to Batman or Pa Cartwright!

Chapter 27

A TRIP TO THE PARK

MY PASTIMES WERE SITTING AT the coffee table in the living room drawing with a pencil and paper, playing Barbie dolls or house or going to the park with my cousins.

My friends and I would make Barbie houses out of pocketbooks we found around the house and have pretend marriages and love affairs between them. My mom was always curious as to why we had to have a bedroom with a door on it and why we needed a bed in the Barbie house. It made her uncomfortable. I couldn't understand why.

I suppose she thought I was naughty because of the masturbating incident that had happened so long before. However, it never occurred to me at the time that she was implying that the beds were for something other than sleeping.

I'd say to my mom, "The Barbies need a door on their bedroom so they can get some peace at night away from their pesky children, and they have to sleep at night to be able to start a new day!"

If it was nice outside, our moms would insist that we all go and play outside. My cousins and I would go bicycling and go to the park together if that was the case.

I was riding my bicycle and my cousin Linda was walking beside me on our way to the park one day. The town had a small park with two merry-go-rounds, a long steel slide and a swing set. The playground was right beside the Catholic church.

There was a big standard-breed poodle locked up in a fenced yard that we had to walk by to get to the park. The poodle's name was Buttons. We'd heard rumours that Buttons was vicious and that he had bitten someone, and now he had to be chained by the neck and fenced up in his backyard.

Linda and I were walking to the park and had to walk by Buttons. We felt safe knowing that he was tied and fenced. We started taunting the huge poodle that stood taller than we did on all fours.

"Buttons, Buttons," we yelled together, laughing.

It wasn't 10 seconds before Buttons jumped over the fence and was running toward us, jumping and barking fiercely. I started peddling, and Linda started running as fast as we could toward the park to get up on the merry-go-round, where we would be safe.

Buttons was too fast for us; he caught Linda by the shoulder with his teeth and brought her down to the pavement. He had her pinned there.

This was the first and only time I had ever been able to climb to the very top of the big merry-go-round. As I swung from the steel bars that held it together, I yelled, "Help, help!"

I watched, hanging from the merry-go-round, as Linda was mauled by Buttons. I felt like I was in a horror movie. It seemed to take so long before anyone came to save her. I knew I couldn't get the dog off of her, and I felt so guilty and so helpless.

A neighbour lady and the dog's owner finally heard our screams and ran out to release Linda from the clutches of the vicious dog. They had to hold the dog back with all their strength to keep him off of Linda.

When the dog was restrained, I felt safe enough to come down from the top of the merry-go-round. Linda was in shock. The neighbour lady held Linda in her arms while I ran to Linda's house to get her mom and dad.

Aunty Evelyn and Uncle Harvey and I came back to Linda immediately, and so did half of the population of Nairn. I explained what had happened to us, while Linda cried and held on to her father in terror. I knew that she had been afraid for her life.

Linda had to be taken to the hospital and given all kinds of needles in her stomach to prevent her from getting rabies. The needles, she told me, were very painful.

Buttons was removed from his owner's house and put to death.

I felt very guilty about Linda's misfortune for a long time after that. I wondered if everyone thought I was a coward for leaving Linda there with the dog like I did. But Linda didn't hold it against me, and I was happy about that.

The whole town thought Linda was brave and lucky to have come away with so few scars. We all were happy to see Buttons gone at last. He had always been a terror for anyone walking by his house. It was a terrible lesson. Everyone but Linda was better off because of it.

Chapter 28

SHOT IN THE HEAD

AUNTY MARIE WAS THE LEADER of my Brownie troop—"Brown Owl," we called her. I was allowed to join the Brownies when I was only six in 1969, too young to even be a "Tweeny." Tweeny was a name they gave the beginner Brownies. I was allowed only because my Aunty Marie was the leader, and she said I could join.

I got to learn all the mottos and sayings that went with being a Brownie. One of the sayings was, "On my honour, I pledge to do my best, to do my duty, to God, the Queen and my country."

All the Brownies were given the task of writing something—a poem or a song for the troop. My mom helped me, and we wrote this: "I'm a little Brownie short and fat, here is my uniform, here's my hat!"

Aunty Marie thought it was wonderful and funny.

I got to bring all the Brownies on a ski trip to my camp one winter. My father had torn down the old canvas shack and put up a three-bedroom cottage. There were no longer any canvas walls with Band-Aids covering all the holes. You couldn't see the ground through the cracks in the floorboards anymore. We didn't have to worry about snakes under our beds or chipmunks in the sugar jar when we returned each spring.

The new cottage was insulated and had an oil furnace in it. It was nice and safe and cozy, but it had lost the ambiance that the old shack had. All of the rustic primitive things that came with the old shack were no longer there. It was sad to change from the old to the new.

With the other Brownies trailing behind me, we skied our way into my cottage from the highway where we left the cars. I played the leader because I knew the way, even though Brown Owl had a camp right beside mine and knew the way just as well.

Aunty Marie's camp was not insulated, and it did not have a stove that could keep us warm enough for a winter night. So I got the privilege of having the Brownies as my guests.

Another time, in the summer, our Brownie group went to Aunty Marie's camp. It still had that rustic feeling; her camp did not yet have all of the modern things that our cottage had now.

For the summer Brownie trip, my parents were at the cottage at the same time. I got to see my mom and dad and Brian and Brenda every day. It was fun to sleep with the Brownies knowing my mom was right next door.

We had sing-alongs by a campfire on the beach, swam and played games in the sand. We had scavenger hunts and did Brownie routines while we were there.

All the Brownies were playing on the beach one late afternoon. My brother, Brian, was outside shooting with a BB gun. He was shooting at the steel barrels that held the earth up around the hillside of the beach.

He shot twice, and somehow the second shot ricocheted off the barrels on the beach and hit me smack dab just above my nose, between the middle of the eyes on my forehead. I fell to the ground in shock.

It stung like crazy, and I didn't know what had hit me. Then I remembered the sound of the gunshot, and I realized it had to have been Brian's gun. I put my hand up to my forehead to check for blood. I searched for the hole or bits of brain matter. I thought I must be dead or dying.

But no, I seemed okay. I could still see, and I could still move, and there was no blood. I got up shaking and weak at the knees, and I looked for Brian on the beach.

When I saw him standing there with his gun in his hand, pretending to be completely unaware of what he'd done, I was stunned. I yelled, "You shot me! How could you? You tried to kill me! I'm telling Mom!"

He ran after me into our camp, yelling, "No, Poochie, it was an accident!"

Mom scolded him good and took his gun away. He told her he didn't even aim it at me. But the spot on my forehead and the big lump coming up said differently. I was in awe thinking that he could shoot me like that.

The Brownies all came over later to my cottage to check and see if I was all right. Mom said I was very lucky to have had the BB miss my eyes and that I would be staying home with her and Dad for the rest of the trip.

I lay on the big bed in Mom and Dad's room with a cold facecloth on the growing lump on my forehead while I heard Brian getting heck like crazy.

It hurt my feelings more than anything. I couldn't believe he would shoot me.

As Dad discovered later, it was true that Brian hadn't really shot me on purpose. He was shooting at the barrels, and the BB ricocheted off them and hit me. Dad found the dents in the barrels to prove it.

My mom had to explain it to me. I was so upset to think Brian could hate me that much. I didn't want to feel that I would have to be afraid for my life because Brian might try to kill me again. I was pretty relieved when Brian showed great remorse for having almost killed me.

Brian was sincere and afraid of having hurt me. He was very nice to me for the entire week after. He cared for me after all. I was grateful to know it.

The Brownies told me that it wasn't as much fun when I wasn't there, and I wasn't there a lot after that trip.

I hated committing to anything. As soon as there was an agreement or a contract made, I felt pressure and wanted out. I guess it was because it reminded me of the pressure I felt when I was committed to school in Grade 1.

Mom would try to convince me to go to Brownies. She would tell me I needed to finish things that I started, I couldn't just quit in the middle of things.

I started to think that maybe she was right—and I didn't want to get involved in anything else again.

Chapter 29

BRENDA

MY SISTER, BRENDA, AND I didn't spend much time together. She would always have a boyfriend over when Mom and Dad were out of town.

Brian always hated Brenda's choice of boyfriends. They were always very loud and aggressive, just like Brian was. Brian and Brenda used to hang out at home a lot, and I suppose Brian was jealous when some boy came in and took her attention away from him.

One of Brenda's boyfriends, Tom, and Brian were always on each other's nerves, and they got into a squabble. Tom stabbed Brian in the hand with a knife.

Brenda was mad at Brian. Mom and Dad and I didn't know anything about Brian's hand and the whole episode until Brenda broke up with Tom a few weeks later.

Then Brian told Brenda and us, "Tom was an ass, and I'm glad that the guy is out of our lives. We didn't need a violent guy like that in our family." That's when he told us that Tom had stabbed him in the hand in a heated argument.

We never knew where Brian's wounds came from. He was often roughhousing, as Mom called it. He got into fights pretty often—sticking up for his pals, he'd say. He was a tough kid, not afraid to fight and loyal to his friends.

Brenda would come off the bus at the bus stop after high school. I would see her getting off of it, and run to her and beg her to let me carry her books home. I wanted to walk with her and keep her company. I would try hard to make her like me. I wanted Brenda and me to be friends. I just wanted her to notice me. Sometimes she would let me carry her books, sometimes she would not. I always thought she was moody.

She ended up getting pregnant when she was 18. It was a very hard time for her. People thought you should not have babies out of wedlock, so she ended up engaged to the baby's father.

Chapter 30

BRIAN

WHEN I WAS ABOUT 9, my brother, Brian, 15 at the time, would sit on top of me on the couch after he and my sister finished washing and drying the dishes, arguing and smacking each other the whole time. It would be my turn for nuggies and wedgies and smacks and teasing. I hated Brian. He taunted me constantly.

Having the school next door meant having its skating rink in my backyard. I would put on my skates, get Dad to pull the laces up nice and tight for me so that I wasn't wobbly and walk over to the rink to skate. I wasn't a great skater, but I was fast. The only thing I couldn't do was stop. I'd crash into the boards to stop, and when I skated fast I would almost knock myself out hitting them so hard.

Brian and his friends often hung out in the rink shack. There were bleachers to sit on and an electric heater to keep warm. I went into the rink shack to get warmed up halfway through the evening, and I caught Brian smoking in there with his friends.

"I'm telling, I'm telling," I yelled at him when I saw the stream of smoke coming from the cigarette in his hand and the letter Os he was trying to make with the smoke from his mouth. He hadn't seen me walk in; he had his face up toward the ceiling and was too busy trying to perfect this new O-making feat.

Wow, this is some real ammunition, I thought.

Brian skated all evening doing circles around me, trying to bribe me into not telling Mom and Dad about what he tried to make me believe was his one and only experience with cigarettes.

He got my attention when he offered me a quarter for my silence. You could buy a pop and a chip and still get a small brown bag full of two-penny candies with 25 cents.

I took it and agreed to be quiet, and he finally left me alone so I could skate. He treated me a little better from then on.

My mom and dad smoked at the time, and I was repulsed by the smell of our house because of it. The smoke made their clothes smell dirty; it turned the ceiling, white lampshades and everything else white in the house into an icky shade of yellow. I would beg them to quit. Nag them all the time. But they would ignore me.

We created a pool for the hockey games whenever the Maple Leafs were on TV. The pool would get handed all around town. We offered each neighbour a chance to buy a ticket.

Everyone would pick a piece of paper. They would pay a price for it, and the money went into a hat. If the paper they had chosen had the correct scores at the end of the game, they would win the money in the hat.

I was often chosen to bring the hat around to sell the tickets because I hated watching the games. If I had to sit and watch hockey, I was a pest. Every time there was any kind of a sport game on TV, I would complain. I hated watching all sports, with a passion.

I wasn't good in sports at school. When it was time to do a quarter-mile run, it would get so difficult, I'd have a hard time breathing, I would get overwhelmed, and I would end up choking and throwing up. I would see stars and know that if I didn't squat down I would pass out, so having to run terrified me. Later on in my life, I found out I had asthma.

I couldn't run, and I was never picked by the teams for any sports. I was always a leftover, the last one to be picked. I'm sure the teams thought they were stuck with me at the end of picking people.

There were a couple of other kids who were not always chosen too. We didn't care about the games; we didn't really want to play anyway. In a baseball game, we'd be way off in the field picking daisies or talking. We wouldn't even see the ball when it finally came our way.

Though I hated sports, I loved getting involved with the hockey betting pool because everyone would want a chance to win. Now and then, I'd buy a ticket with my allowance, and then I would find the game a little more interesting, at least near the end. I won the pot once; the winnings were about two hundred dollars, which was an awful lot of money to me.

My mom bet a friend she was watching a hockey game with fifty dollars that she could quit smoking and that he could not quit. He put his fifty dollars in and said, "Okay, first one to smoke loses their money."

My dad decided to quit too. He thought it would be better and easier for them both to quit together. Mom washed everything that week—the walls, the pillows and the blankets. Our house smelled so fresh and had white things in it again.

I didn't have to open my window every time Mom lit up a cigarette in the car anymore. Mom was always cold; she hated that I would open the window when she smoked. She'd accuse me of trying to freeze her out! Between the heat, the smoke and the asthma, I really opened my window just to be able to breathe.

I was so happy when they quit smoking.

However, Mom started smoking again after having quit for about two years. She ran into the man she'd made the bet with at the grocery store, and she told him she was a smoker again and paid him her fifty dollars.

The man took the money; we all heard that he started smoking again too. I don't know if he started before my mom did, but he did take her money. I was always kind of sceptical about him after that.

"Brian smokes," I told my mom after she had started again. I thought it might make her feel guilty enough to quit again. Brian was 16, and I figured it had been kept a secret long enough. How long would Brian have expected me to keep it quiet for a quarter anyway?

"How do you know that Brian smokes?" Mom asked.

"I caught him in the rink shack, and he paid me a quarter not to tell," I explained.

Mom was angry. She told me, "You'd better give Brian his quarter back now that you tattled on him!"

Brian was always out with his friends, and they were always into some kind of trouble. They would loiter where they weren't supposed to, smoke cigarettes, sell marijuana, taunt and tease all the younger kids who were good kids. There was always all kinds of badass stuff they could find for themselves to get into.

Mom thought he was her angel. *Li'l altar boy my ass*, I thought. I was tired of hearing how perfect he was. I knew it wasn't so. Telling on him somehow brought me restitution for all the picking on me he did. But it really disappointed Mom, and that made me feel awful for having said anything. Plus she thought I should give him the quarter back, which I didn't have anymore!

When Brian found out that I'd told Mom on him and got him into trouble for smoking, he and the rest of his friends in Nairn labelled me a snitch and a vulture. They would continuously call me that and mock me whenever they saw me.

It bugged me for a while, but I just stopped regarding them at all. When they realized it was having no effect on me, they stopped and we all got over it.

Brian started hanging out in town later at night. He would stay out way past curfew. He seemed to try to get into trouble after Mom and Dad found out he smoked.

One night, Brian came home after we were all asleep. He made himself a bologna and ketchup sandwich in the kitchen, took a bite and passed out—fainted and fell.

My dad and mom and I were awakened by the bang when Brian's body hit the floor.

My mom walked into the kitchen fearfully behind Dad. They were originally thinking maybe there was a robber in the house. They saw Brian lying on the floor with the knife in his hand. Mom thought there was blood all over his face. She was hysterical. "Rog, Rog, Rog!" she screamed.

Dad walked up to Brian and picked him up from off of the floor. Brian was stoned on marijuana and delirious. Dad was ready to kill my brother when he realized that Brian had probably smoked too much pot.

This event with Brian passing out in the kitchen late at night happened again, and then my parents decided to give him an ultimatum to either quit smoking pot or move out. He chose to move out and live with some of his badass friends in town.

Brian would come around to visit sometimes because he'd get lonely. I remember Mom being angry and hurt and not talking to him.

I said to Mom one day that I missed him. "Why?" she asked. "All you and Brian did was fight. I would think you would be happy to have him gone!"

I said to her, "But now I have no one to fight with!"

Brian stayed with his friends at one of their houses and got a summer job to support himself. He came around with a girl he picked up while he was away on holidays. He said that she was his little souvenir from the Sault. He had met her while he was partying in Sault Saint Marie on the weekend with his friends.

He told me he wanted to keep her, and that she was staying with him at his pal's house. She was okay, kind of dumb; she had the biggest boobs I ever did see.

Brian ended up sending her back to the Sault on the Greyhound bus within only two weeks. Maybe she had to go because Brian's pal never really wanted the extra mouth to feed.

I guessed Brian probably got bored of those boobs being her only asset. She wasn't much of a talker.

I was glad that Brian got rid of her anyway, because Mom and Dad said she wasn't welcome at our house. I missed him, and I hoped he would make it up with Mom and Dad and move back home. I hated my family not being together anymore. I never wanted things to change from the way they were in the past. Even if all Brian and I did was fight, I wanted him to come back.

Chapter 31

BRENDA'S WEDDING

I WAS NOT INCLUDED IN Brenda's wedding party in the spring of 1972. I thought she would ask me to be a bridesmaid or a flower girl. But she'd already planned it all with her friends, and there was no room for me. "You're too old to be a flower girl anyway," she said to me. I was 10.

When the wedding was in the planning stages, Brenda's sister-in-law-to-be came over to our house. She helped me put makeup on. She told me she thought I was very pretty. She was so kind to me. She understood how hurt I was when I told her that I felt left out. She helped find me something to do so that I could be useful and feel important. I was going to mind the guest book and make sure everyone signed it.

The day of the wedding came, and Brenda looked beautiful. I remember Dad talking to her before we got in the car to go to the church.

"You know, you don't have to do this if you don't want to," Dad said with tears in his eyes.

Brenda looked back at him with tears in her eyes too and said, "I know, Dad, thank you, but I do want to do this!" Dad put the car into gear and we headed to the church.

The wedding party was huge. All of the girls were dressed in purple crushed-velvet dresses with little hoods on them. I wished I'd gotten to wear a purple dress too and stand up beside Brenda. I wished I had meant something to her and that we were closer to one another. I would miss all the opportunities to get closer to her now that she'd be moving out.

The church was bright and alive with relatives from everywhere. There were flowers and ribbons on everything. Mom cried at the church. "Is getting married a bad thing?" I asked Mom. "What is wrong, why aren't you happy?"

"It's just hard to let her go," Mom said. "I'll miss her!"

Chapter 32

POETRY

I HATED THINGS TO CHANGE, and I found it constantly happening and very hard to deal with. I'd become depressed about things that were happening around me all the time.

Maybe it was teenage hormones causing my problems. I'd been getting emotional about everything. I wanted everything to return to the way it used to be, when we were all happy and living together. I missed being a little kid and cuddling with my mom. I missed Brenda's living at home and Brian's constant taunting and teasing.

I sat down one evening and found that there were words in my mind that I needed to write down on paper. I wanted them written before I forgot them. I sat and wrote this poem:

You're just a babe
And your life is quite wild
Until you're all grown up
And no longer a child

You'll try to make
The best parts last
But get lost in the future
Forgetting the past

There are times to come
With decisions to make
New ropes to learn
And new turns to take

So don't get lost
In those sudden hopes
Just take all the turns
And learn all the ropes

In the times to come
You'll remember the pain
Only to find
You're beginning again.

I loved writing poems and stories. I found that writing could help me to release my thoughts. Mom said to me, "Poochie, you think too much all the time!"

It became therapeutic for me to sit and put all of my thoughts down on paper and make a story of them. Writing helped me to rid myself of any anxiety I was feeling. I started my writing by making a diary. I wrote everything I felt and did in it every night before bed.

Brenda had her first baby in the summer of 1972, not long after her wedding, a girl she named Lee. Lee was beautiful, tiny and gentle. I loved her like she was my own baby. She was the best thing to come into my life that summer. I loved it when they brought Lee to visit us.

I would entertain Lee with toys and games. I'd get to snuggle her to sleep and help her eat and bathe. I would lay with Lee in my bed because Brenda would let her sleep with me when they came to visit.

I would play with her hair and brush it through my fingers until her eyes would start to close, and within minutes she would fall fast asleep.

Brenda always wondered, "How do you get her to sleep so fast?"

I just loved her, and I had so much patience and interest in her.

I thought that if Brenda would give her to me, I would keep her in a heartbeat, if Mom would let me. But the opportunity for me to keep Lee never came. Brenda and her husband moved about 50 miles away from Nairn, and sometimes it felt like ages before she would bring Lee back to see us.

Every time I would get to see Lee again she would be bigger and older, and I realized that little people sure do grow fast.

A baby boy that Brenda and her husband named Rudy was born a year after Lee. I didn't get to know Rudy very well because their visits to our house, and us to their house, became fewer and fewer with time.

My parents didn't like Brenda's husband. They thought he was boisterous and mean to Brenda.

Chapter 33

PORT ELGIN

I N NAIRN, THERE WAS A pulp and paper mill that my father worked at for a while. He didn't have to travel five minutes to go to work at the mill. He soon started working in the mines surrounding us because there was more money to be made in hard-rock mining.

My dad enjoyed the work in the mines, and he was always a leader of some sort. The work that he did there was very dangerous. That was why "I make the big bucks," he'd say. He worked over his head with a jackhammer, drilling and digging upward and outward. He'd make the tunnel in which the other men would mine for coal or nickel or gold.

Dad would have opportunities to become a foreman or a boss. He would regretfully have to turn them down. The possibility of the other men finding out he was illiterate was shameful and embarrassing to him.

He could read a tiny bit; he knew some words in English just as I did in French. My mom would try to teach him, but he was really not interested in changing his ways. He figured he was too old to learn. "You can't teach an old dog new tricks," he'd say.

He sure liked to complain about his disability and hated having to pass up opportunities when they arose. Dad was pretty stubborn, I guess.

When I was in Grade 5 in the spring of 1973, a really good job offer came to Dad from far away, in a place called Douglas Point. He was going to get a chance to make a lot of money. He didn't have to be educated because it was a hard-rock mining opportunity that he was accustomed to.

My mom and dad did not tell me right away. They really didn't feel I should have any bearing on their decision to move or not. They wanted to spare me the aggravation, in case they decided not to even go.

It wasn't until the decision was final and we were going to move that they told me. I usually hated anything to change, and they expected I would be unhappy and difficult about it once I knew. But I was so excited to leave Nairn. It was going to be the first time we'd ever moved away anywhere else. I couldn't wait to pack up and go. There was nobody to miss in Nairn anymore. Mom and Dad were very surprised at my reaction.

We packed up our belongings in boxes and rented our house. I remember driving out of Nairn looking back at the old town through the truck window. Good riddance, I thought. I was not going to miss this place at all.

We moved ourselves to a cottage in Port Elgin, and I ended Grade 5 at a new school. I savoured the changes that came with the move. I looked forward to a new house, new friends and a new school, everything new.

The little cottage Dad had found for us was pink on the outside. It had a kitchen and living room together, three bedrooms and a bathroom. There was a big wraparound deck and huge trees down both sides of the street. It looked like a fairy-tale setting.

The appliances and cupboards were old, but my mom dressed them up with clean water or paint. There was no bathtub, just a shower. My mom spent a day and a half scrubbing it out.

The closets were just made of plywood, and they were not very sturdy. I was sleeping in my room one night and the whole closet came down in a sliding pile of boards right beside me. Dad had kept his axe up on the top shelf, and it hit the floor right beside my bed.

It scared the heck out of me. We all jumped, and Mom and Dad ran in from the living room to see what had happened. My face was pale as I pointed at the ax. I was thinking that maybe there was a ghost in the room, and it was trying to kill me.

It took a while to calm me down. Mom just made the bed up in the spare room and put me in there to sleep for the night. I didn't like sleeping in the spare room because there would be a whole room between me and my parents. I thought I was too far away from them to be safe.

Dad fixed the closet the next day, and it was better than it ever was. My dad could fix anything. He would fix our kitchen appliances, radios, blow-dryers, curling irons and anything electrical. Dad could build anything we wanted too.

My mother always knew what it was going to take to make a place feel like home. She was good at decorating and buying things to match. The whole place was really filthy when we moved in. Mom and I worked really hard scrubbing and cleaning, and it didn't take long for it to feel nice. Dad started in his new job right away.

Brian stayed in Nairn. He was 16 and living with some of his badass friends. He'd found a job as a cook in a men's work camp for the summer. He bought an orange motorcycle, and he was really growing up fast without us.

Brian came to see us once in Port Elgin. He was nice to me the whole time he was around. I wondered what the heck had happened to him.

I thought maybe he was dying or something like that. He even gave me a gift, a twenty-dollar bill. For no reason, he said, just because he missed me.

I felt a little skeptical about taking his money. I took it and waited for the catch, but there really wasn't any. I don't know what happened to him to have changed him so much, but I liked the new him.

Brian didn't stay long in Port Elgin with us, but Mom and Dad made sure that when he went back to Nairn, he had a place to stay. They got him a room to board in at a friend's home back in Nairn. Mom and Dad paid for Brian to stay there and to be taken care of and safe. Mom and Dad wanted him to finish his Grade 12. I was happy we were all friends again. I was glad the fighting between my parents and Brian was over.

Starting school in a new place was fun. Everyone was so nice to me. I made friends, but most of them were not as easy to get to as the friends I'd had in Nairn. Everyone lived much farther apart, and some of the kids were even bussed to school.

I loved Port Elgin. It had a theatre and a main street with more stores on it than Espanola had. I could walk to the theatre to see the movies by myself.

My best friend was a French girl named Suzanne. She lived in a cottage to the rear of ours, and her dad worked in the mine with my dad. She was really French, and they spoke French at her house. I never understood anything they said. They could not speak English at all. Only Suzanne was bilingual.

We spent winter in Port Elgin, and the snow came in like it was never going to end. "It came in like a lion," my mom said. I couldn't believe the amount of snow we got. I'd never ever seen that much snow in my whole life. It all came in a matter of 24 hours. Snow so thick and heavy you couldn't see your hand in front of your face while you were outside in it.

The next day after the big storm, a lot of the kids in town were outside playing. We were digging our way out of our houses. We would try to walk on the top of the snow and fall deep into it. We were jumping off each other's rooftops. The snow was just awesome and amazing.

My parents went everywhere by snow machine that week. School got cancelled for days. It was really fun. I spent the whole time either at Suzanne's house or her at mine. Winter was certainly a fun season living in the Southern winter snow belt.

My father would bring really beautiful and interesting rocks home from the mine for me. They were rocks with crystals that were purple and pink pointing up from them. I imagined it must be like a dream world walking around in the mine with all the pink and purple crystals poking down and shining at you.

One time when Dad got home I was so excited to see what he had brought. I was lying on the couch with my feet up the back of it, watching TV. Dad came in through the front door.

I somersaulted backward to get off the couch and completely lost my breath. It was terrifying. Mom and Dad kept moving me and trying to get me to breathe again. I just wasn't able to get it back. It lasted for about 30 seconds, but it sure scared us all.

It must have been the way I fell off the couch with my head tucked under my neck. It knocked the wind out of me. I got some colour back in my face and returned to normal after my breath came back. My dad had a whole lunch pail full of purple rocks to give to me.

Now and then, Mom and Dad and I would pack for a weekend, and we would take a trip back to Nairn to visit. The kids in the old town were so interested in what I had been doing and where I had been. I felt like a celebrity.

We went back to Port Elgin afterward, and I felt like there was a great empty void in my life. I felt like I was suddenly not really at home in Port Elgin. I was missing Nairn.

My mother and father felt the void too. Mom and I would be in tears every time we talked about Nairn and our old home.

Mom was very lonely for Brian and for her family who lived near us when we were living in Nairn. I believe Dad was lonesome too, even though he would never admit it. I knew that Dad would do whatever it took to keep my mom happy. It didn't take long. After one of our visits back, we began our plans to return to live in Nairn.

Chapter 34

RETURNED TO SENDER

MY FATHER GOT WORK AT the mines in Northern Ontario again in 1974. While he was working, we moved back to Nairn.

I was upset to have to leave Suzanne, but I thought we could keep in touch forever. We lasted about three months writing back and forth to each other. I don't know if her family left Port Elgin or what happened. It made me feel really sad when our correspondence stopped. I would send her letters, and she would not send me a reply.

Then my own letters started being returned to me. I would complain to my mom, and Mom would just say, "Things change, life goes on, you have to move on too!"

"Change, change, change," I would complain. "I hate it!"

Our old house was occupied when we wanted to return, so my father bought an old fixer-upper house on Hall Street. It was about two blocks from the school and 50 feet from the post office and general store. Dad also purchased the lot beside the old house. He planned to eventually build a brand new dream house on the empty lot. The old house was only going to be a temporary home for us.

I loved the old house. It had no basement and two bedrooms, one of which Brian took when he moved back in with us. The other bedroom was for my parents.

It felt so nice to have Brian back home. He started going back to high school again, and it was like old times, although Brian would not be home a lot in the evenings or on the weekends. Mom and Dad seemed to be okay with his being out a lot now. I guess he had stopped smoking, and Mom was just glad to have him living in our home again.

My bed was put at the top of the stairway above the furnace. The furnace was an oil furnace, and it was kind of stinky. I thought it would be hard to get used to the smell of the oil, but I did in a matter of days. The smell started to become what "home" would smell like to me after that.

My "room"—really, it was meant to be a foyer at the top of the stairs and not a bedroom at all—was decorated with blue and white stripes. The stripes would make me nauseated when I lay in bed trying to look at them. They would make me dizzy. I learned to ignore them. Mom told me one time that they made her dizzy when she looked at them too.

Everyone had to walk by me when they went to bed. Still, I liked my little space; I never felt like I was alone for long. I just didn't have a door to close.

If I was still awake, I could have conversations with Mom just like we were sleeping in the same room. But my mom and dad would sometimes close their bedroom door at night, and I would feel abandoned. They said, "If the bedroom door is closed, stay out!"

I felt really alone on those nights, but often Mom would open the door up again later because their room would get cold when they closed their door. There were no vents into their bedroom, so the furnace couldn't blow any warm air into their room. The door being open was the only way for them to get heat in there.

If I couldn't sleep and the door was left open between us, I would stay awake talking to them. I think they would get tired of me. They would tell me, "That's enough, Poochie, we're not going to be listening anymore. We need to go to sleep."

I liked to sing in bed, too, and they would often yell to me that they'd had enough, and I'd have to sing more quietly until I fell asleep.

The old house was colder than most of the houses we lived in. There weren't as many vents, and there was no basement—just a crawl space made of dirt that you could enter from a door inside of the bathroom.

There was only one bathroom for all of us. That made it very hard to get ready for school in the morning, with everyone else needing to use the toilet. Mom would get up early, always, and start her housework, and the laundry appliances were in the bathroom too.

We wore mom's hand-knitted sweaters, mitts and hats, and of course all the great afghans and quilts that my mom and grandma made helped to keep us toasty.

It was fun coming back to Nairn and going back to my old school. Everybody seemed to be so happy to see me and have me back. My old friends and I just picked up where we left off. I felt at home once more.

Brian's changes in personality stuck. He stayed nice to me. Having him around got to be really nice. It was weird having him there with us acting differently than he used to, but it was nice to have him there nevertheless.

I always wondered what made him change into this new person he'd become. I prayed for these nice changes to stick with him.

Chapter 35

MS. LACHANCE

WHEN THE NEW SCHOOL YEAR started in Grade 7, September of 1974, we got a new teacher at Nairn Public School. Her name was Ms. Lachance. She took lots of time with each of us kids individually. Ms. Lachance was very gentle and patient. I loved being in her class. She made me feel so special.

About two weeks before the end of the school year and the beginning of summer vacation, we were going to take imaginary visits to different places each day for a week.

Ms. Lachance was friends with Miss Baker. Miss Baker was a supply teacher who would help the other teachers out. Normally she taught French. Ms. Lachance and Miss Baker would stay after school, and they would not leave until the classroom was decorated with the theme of the country that we were going to be pretending to visit the next day.

We had France Day, and everything was French. We had to speak French. We prepared and ate French food. We had a picture of the Eiffel Tower and other French places up on the wall. We wore beret hats for the day.

The next day was Mexican Day, and we had sombreros and striped colourful blankets to wear as ponchos. We had piñatas to hit and Mexican tacos and nachos that we prepared ourselves. We played Mexican games, and it was the most fun we'd ever had in school.

Usually, the last couple weeks of school were spent reviewing what we had learned during the year. This was much more fun, like going to a big party.

Ms. Lachance was more like our friend than our teacher. I would go home and tell Mom about Ms. Lachance, and Mom could see how Ms. Lachance's teaching was affecting my interest in school and learning. I was doing great that year.

The morning after our Mexican Day at school, we were all sitting at our desks. We were waiting for Ms. Lachance and Miss Baker to come into the class after the bell rang, but they did not. We knew they traveled from Espanola to Nairn together every morning in the same car to get to school. We just assumed they were late.

Our principal came into our class that morning. The whole classroom was trying to keep quiet. We were giggling and wondering what kind of surprise Ms. Lachance and Miss Baker would have planned for us that day.

The principal didn't look at us like he normally did. He had a very concerned look on his face, and he sat down in front of the class on Ms. Lachance's desk. With a very sad look on his face, he started to speak, and he told us that on the way to school, Ms. Lachance and Miss Baker were involved in a fatal car accident at the bridge coming out of McKerrow. Ms. Lachance was driving. She lost control of the car and hit a rock cliff. Ms. Lachance was killed instantly.

Miss Baker was hurt pretty badly, but she would survive. She was in the hospital. She would not be coming back to school again until the next school year.

I was in shock. My eyes welled up with tears, as did many of the other children's. We cried, and we didn't want to believe it could be true. I couldn't believe it. I felt like I was in a bad dream. My ears were ringing, and I felt like I was going to pass out or die.

Our class was dismissed that day right after we'd been given the news. I went home devastated. I couldn't stop crying, and I just couldn't believe Ms. Lachance could be gone forever.

I walked back into the house that morning, and I guess my mom had already heard. She opened her arms to me with a very sad look. I walked into them and cried. Mom knew how much Ms. Lachance meant to me. She did her best to comfort me.

I think I was in denial for about a week after hearing the news. I could not understand how she could have been there one day and completely gone the next.

I went over the day before in my head again and again. The fun we'd had with Mexican Day. Laughing and being so excited for the next excursion together. How could she do this to us? Why didn't she fight to live? Why was Miss Baker alive and not her?

I was very depressed. I felt like I was on a roller coaster and I had no control of anything.

The walls could just crumble and fall down around my feet at any moment. I couldn't understand how life could just end and people could just be gone. Gone, gone, where did they go?

My mom was very understanding. She tried to comfort me. She tried to help keep me distracted. She let me stay home from school for the next week until summer holidays. I don't think I could have functioned anyway. I didn't want to go back to the school or the classroom without Ms. Lachance there anymore.

I was very angry that Miss Baker didn't die instead of Ms. Lachance. When Miss Baker taught me the next school year, I held a great resentment toward her.

Losing Ms. Lachance was the most painful thing I had ever experienced in my childhood up until then. It took a long time for the pain of her loss to fade. That summer was the loneliest summer vacation ever. It took many days and nights of crying until, finally, somehow, I started to move on and forget.

It took everything inside of me not to let go of her. I didn't want to forget her. I thought she must be looking down at me. How could she forgive me if I were ever to forget her? She was so special to me.

Life does continue somehow, and gradually, your mind stops getting lured back into the grief. First it was hard to let go of her, and then it became hard to hang on to her any longer. I will never forget her completely. I miss her.

Chapter 36

MORE BAD NEWS

M Y PARENTS WERE OUT AT a friend's house in Nairn and I was 13, at home, playing with my cousin Debbie. We were listening to her new Elton John records in the living room when the phone rang. It was a lady looking for my parents.

"Is this the residence of Roger and Annette Marcoux?" she asked.

"Yes," I replied, thinking, *Oh gee, a telemarketer calling to sell something.* I was ready to hang up on her.

"It's very important that I speak with one of them," the lady on the other end of the line said.

"They are not home," I explained. "Can I take a message?"

She asked me if Brenda Marcoux was related to me.

I replied, "Yes, she is my sister!"

The lady said that all she could tell me over the phone was that Brenda Marcoux and her husband and her two children had been in a car accident, and they had been taken to the Espanola Hospital.

"Oh my God," I said, "are they okay?"

She said, "Just please get your parents to call or come to the hospital as soon as you can."

I was so afraid. Were Brenda and the kids okay? Were they alive?

It was not good news. I was numb. I wanted to know more, but the hospital people would not tell me anything else.

Debbie took one look at me and said, "Let's go find your mom and dad!"

"I know where they are," I said.

We peddled our bikes to my parents' friend's house. I ran in and was so happy to see that they were there. I told them what I'd heard. Within seconds, we were in the car, and I waved good-bye to Debbie. We drove hurriedly to the Espanola Hospital to be with Brenda and her family.

The nurse took my mom and dad aside. She told them that Brenda was alive, but she had a lot of damage done to her face and was about to go into surgery. My mom told me to wait in the lobby, and she and Dad went in alone to see Brenda. I paced back and forth, scared and wondering what was happening.

Mom and Dad finally came out looking very pale. My mom was shaky. She was crying, and she looked weak.

"How is Brenda?" I asked. "Can I go in and see her?"

Mom shook her head as if to say *Brenda is not good.* Mom said she didn't want me to go into Brenda's hospital room. "You will be afraid," Mom said.

"No I won't, Mom, I'm okay, I want to see her!" Now I was really afraid, but curious. I begged and begged, thinking that I might never see her alive again by the way they were talking.

Mom finally gave up fighting with me and told me, "Just go and see her then!"

I walked into Brenda's hospital room, and she was in a bed that had her sitting up. She wore a green hospital gown and had a lot of blood on her face and hands.

She did not look like our Brenda. All of her teeth were broken off into shards. The skin on her chin was ripped back to her neck; her nose was cut and half of it was on the side of her face. Her eyes were black and blue and red. She had broken parts of her body that I didn't even know the names of. She was very distraught.

She looked at me like she didn't know me. She was asking everyone for her children.

"Where are my children?" she'd scream. She was on medication, and it made her delirious. She didn't even recognize me. She ignored me and she looked possessed, I thought.

I ran out of her room. "She's not okay," I cried to Mom. "She didn't even know me!" I tried to be strong, but I had to leave the room. I felt nauseated and saw stars, and I had to get away before I passed out. I had to sit down and try to prevent myself from fainting, because fear was all I could feel and it was overwhelming me.

"The doctors were just here, they said she will be okay," Mom said. "I told you it would be hard to see her. She was hurt badly. The doctors are not sure about the baby or Lee right now."

"She asked for the kids," I said to Mom. "She wants to know if they are okay!"

"She will be asleep shortly. She'll be better off that way for the time being," Mom explained.

Life was so fragile. I was again realizing how quickly everything can be taken away.

It seemed like such a short time ago that this had just happened to me, having to cope with a great loss. I wanted to cry again, "Why is this happening to me?" It felt so selfish to even think of crying after remembering Brenda and the state she was in.

"We need to find out how Lee and Rudy are doing," Mom said.

We were able to go into the hospital room where Lee was laying, plugged into tubes and IVs. The nurse led us in to see her. She was only three, and she was in a hospital crib in a full body cast with a pin through her right arm and another pin through her right leg.

The pins were there to keep the limbs raised and to prevent her from being able to move her body. She needed to be still so that her bones would set and she could heal properly. She had not yet come into consciousness from the accident. She had stitches on her face and over her eye, and they could not be sure if she had brain damage or not until she woke up.

I was terrified, and my heart felt like it was ready to stop as we waited for her to awaken.

She was so small and innocent, I couldn't imagine God had a reason for taking her from us right now. I stayed by her bed watching her chest go up and down with each breath. I kept looking at her little body so small and so sweet, not believing this whole event, praying, waiting and hoping.

"Lee Lee, it's Aunty Poochie, sweetie, can you hear me?" I kept asking.

Lee finally awoke. She said, "Why am I in a crib? Where is Mommy and Daddy and Rudy?" She didn't like being stuck there in the crib like she was. She wanted to know what was going on, what happened.

Her lips were parched, with dried blood on them. She didn't look like she was in pain. She was a little delirious but mostly frightened and upset as to why or how she'd gotten there.

We all felt great relief to hear her voice.

I was not afraid for her anymore. We called the nurse, and she came to Lee's room immediately. She looked at Lee, did a few quick tests with her and told us she looked really good for what she'd been through. We were so happy to hear that.

But baby Rudy was not out of the woods yet. We went to the intensive-care-unit window. We could not go in and touch him or even breathe his air.

The doctors were worried about the water on his brain and infection and all sorts of things that could cause complications. We just stood and looked at him. Rudy was breathing but asleep. He was not going to wake up any time soon, the nurses said. I decided to walk back to see Lee.

Rudy had been in my sister's lap when they hit the guardrail that morning in the car. We thanked God for the guardrail and the cable that held the car as it was hanging over the water. If the guardrail hadn't been there on that cold winter day, my sister and her whole family would have been swallowed up in the icy water of the Spanish River, and they never would have survived the accident.

They were driving a Camaro, and it had a very light back end. They hit black ice, and the car sped into a fishtail. Then it spun all the way down toward the top of the bridge. The car was found by the police and the ambulance just hanging by the cable over the edge.

Everyone we knew either read about the accident in the paper or heard about it in the news. Everyone said how sorry they were for our pain and that their prayers were with us.

Rudy had been diagnosed with brain damage and was in critical condition in the intensive-care unit. He had water on his brain, the doctors said, and they were draining it to prevent any more damage from the swelling. He lay there with tubes and wires coming all out of him. His whole little head was all bandaged up to hold it together.

The doctors said that his prognosis was not good. Mom told me that if he lived, they as much as said that he'd probably be a vegetable.

My sister was in shock for a long time after the accident. But through her pain from a broken pelvis and a broken arm as well as all of the facial damage, she walked to the intensive-care unit each day to see Rudy and Lee.

She would struggle in pain with crutches holding her up, taking small steps to the floor with the chapel, to pray for Rudy's life. She'd go to his side, hold his hand and just pray. It was a very difficult time for her.

My brother-in-law was not hurt. It was amazing. He had a few scratches and bruises, but that was all. He was in good physical shape. He got to go home.

I felt angry with him. It was bad enough that he was never bringing them to visit us before. Now look what he'd gone and done! Just about took them all right out from under us.

I didn't understand why I felt that way. I just wanted someone to blame for it all.

The only good thing that came from the accident was having the opportunity to have Brenda, Lee and Rudy so close and to be able to go and see them every day.

In the many days to come, I tried to help Lee manage her boredom. Being stuck lying there in the same position for so long in the hospital bed was very difficult for a little girl of three years old. She was bored out of her little mind.

They had a TV in her room and we'd watch cartoons together, but she never got out of bed. Though we would buy and bring her all sorts of toys to brighten her day, what she really wanted was to get out of bed. Lee got very cranky near the end of her stay at the hospital.

Finally, Rudy woke up out of his deep sleep. The doctors had to do tests and more tests to see how well Rudy could function. When all the testing was done and the results were in, the doctors told us that he was going to survive the accident and that his brain looked very promising. But they could not be certain of the extent of brain damage that had been caused until he developed more, with age and growing.

Rudy had a little bald head that looked like it was stitched together like a baseball. His hair would cover the stitches with time.

Brenda was released and had to walk with crutches for a while because of her broken pelvis. She had a hard time, being unable to pick up the baby or Lee. Lee was pretty demanding as well for her. Mom and I went to stay with them for a while, to help Brenda with the kids.

Brenda had all of her teeth pulled out and got dentures. With time, her wounds healed and the scars faded. Her nose and chin repair was done very nicely, and you could hardly tell that anything had ever happened once it had healed.

Lee was happy to be released from the hospital. The casts were still on her leg and her arm. Her arm was still pinned above her head, so she was top-heavy and found it hard to get mobile. She spent lots of time just lying on the couch at her house. She'd cry a lot and get very frustrated.

When she finally got the leg cast removed, she almost had to learn to walk again. Her leg looked sort of green and dead when the cast was gone. There was no muscle left in it, and she had a heck of a time getting her balance. The arm still in a cast didn't help with the balancing act. Her arm took a little longer to heal for some reason.

We were told to just treat Rudy normally, that his head was fully healed and that we had no reason to be overly careful with him. Rudy developed like all normal babies. He learned to eat solid food at a normal age. He could sit up when he was six months old. He learned to walk at around one year old. He looked and acted like your everyday sweet little toddler.

With every milestone Rudy would pass, we were so relieved and happy. He learned and moved on through each step of babyhood right on schedule. With time and visits with him to the hospital, the diagnoses was at last confirmed. Rudy was absolutely healed and normal; there was no brain damage to be found. The doctors and nurses claimed that it was truly a miracle.

The whole family celebrated when we found out the news about Rudy. He was as perfect as he could ever have been. He was growing and developing and learning and understanding just as he should.

Mom and I went back home to Dad. Our help was no longer crucial. Brenda healed just fine and so did Lee, once she got her arm cast off and got her bearings back. They all had a few scars but were stronger for having lived through it.

Chapter 37

A SUMMER JOB

MY DAD BUILT HIS DREAM home in 1975, with help from friends and neighbours, on the property next door. He started it and finished it all within one season. I helped nail the roof trusses. We rented our old house out and moved into the new one. It was beautiful, new and fresh, no more oil furnace smell and my very own room. I had forgotten how nice it was to have a door on my room and privacy.

I was 15 in the summer of 1977, and Brenda had started a new job working as a bartender. Her husband worked in the mines in the day and at the bar with her at night. She mentioned that they could use some help with the kids. They needed a babysitter, and I volunteered to stay over at their house for the summer and help out.

I had so much fun with Lee and Rudy. I would play hide and seek with them, and memory games, and all kinds of fun things to occupy them. Lee was four, and she was at a really fun age. But she was very sneaky and mischievous.

She could climb up on everything. On occasion, you would find her sitting on top of the refrigerator in the kitchen or on top of the highboy dresser in the bedroom. She did not let anything stop her. Sometimes you had to try to figure out how the heck she could have climbed up to where she was sitting.

I would walk into a room where I had just left her, and when I came back, within minutes, she'd be on top of something else. She would nonchalantly and quietly be playing with something that was put up high to keep it away from her, like a bottle of nail polish or matches or candy.

I remember her sticking a bobby pin into an electrical receptacle and getting shocked. She only did that once!

Rudy was quite and sweet and innocent. He followed Lee but never tried all of the antics that she would.

There sure was a lot of work with having little kids. I don't think I had had any idea how much energy and time they demanded. Plus the house needed cleaning, so by the end of the day, I would be exhausted.

It was an eye-opening summer for me. I loved being with Lee and Rudy. I made sure they were happy, fed and clean when Brenda came home.

Now and then, I would be home alone with Brenda and the kids. Brenda did not seem happy. She often looked stressed out to me. I could tell she felt depressed with her life.

One afternoon, Brenda brought me to the bar where she worked. Everyone who knew Brenda loved her. She had a wonderful sense of humour; she could remember every joke that anybody ever told her. She was always happy and fun to be around when she was out of the house.

I felt so grown-up, like I was beginning to be a friend to my sister. I thought it was pretty neat to be inside a bar for the first time. Brenda sat us down at a table and got me a Coke, and we chatted with her work companions. She included me in the conversations as if I were a grown-up, and she bragged about my helping her at home.

For the first time in my life, I really felt that Brenda noticed me. It felt good to have a sister.

Chapter 38

BROKEN VOWS

*B*RENDA HAD ANOTHER BABY BOY, in June of 1978, who she named Joey. He was so cute and quiet. Out of the blue he used to say, "I'm so happy too."

When Joey was around four years old, Brenda would show up at our house on occasion with bruises, crying and very unhappy. We believed that she and her husband were not getting along, and we suspected he'd been hitting her. We went back with her to her house, packed up her things and brought her and the kids home to our house.

I was so excited. I thought they were going to come and live with us.

Brenda's husband was not going to let that happen. They ended up parting, but somehow, in the courts, he was given sole custody of the children. Brenda was devastated. Mom and Dad and I were also confused and hurt.

From what I had heard, her husband was involved with some bad people and had threatened my sister's life. Brenda was afraid of him and would do whatever he told her to. All Brenda would share with us was that it was best for the children and for her welfare that her ex-husband had the kids. We didn't understand what was going on between them, and she would not tell us anything about it.

I don't know how she coped with the loss of her children. She spent most of her time crying. I spent time with her at her new apartment after she moved away again and on her own, and I know she cried most nights for the children and suffered greatly without them.

She would get to see them on occasion, but that was never enough. She'd yell and cry when it was time to leave them again. Her life was in such torment. I think her self-confidence took a turn for the worse, and she lost interest in most everything. Just existing to see the kids when she could and working at the hotel in Nairn.

Brenda, finally, turned to the church for help—which resulted in my mom being very unhappy with the Catholic religion. Brenda went to the priest to try to get the Catholic Church to forgive her for divorcing and allow her to come back into the Church. The Catholics did not believe in divorce. The priest told her that she would have to put in writing and sign that she never loved her husband. Only then could she have her marriage annulled and be allowed back into the Catholic Church.

She could not do that. She told my mom and dad, "I can't lie, Mom. I loved him when I married him. Why else would I have had three children with him?"

My mom was so upset with the Catholic Church for turning its back on Brenda when she needed it, she stopped going to church herself. She felt betrayed and let down by the Catholic system. It caused her much distress.

Chapter 39

ELDERS

BRIAN WAS LEARNING TO PLAY the guitar once we moved back from Port Elgin and he moved back in with us. I love the way it sounded, and we could sing to it together.

Mom and Dad bought me an organ for Christmas, and within a month of getting it, I could play anything anybody asked me to. I guess Brian and I had the Marcoux ear for music.

I thought that maybe Brian and I would have a band together someday. He showed me a little bit of guitar picking, but I found it hurt my fingers too much to do it. The strings were too thick for me to press hard enough to make them play. My fingers were little and arthritic. They would get big gouges in them from the strings. So I stuck to my organ.

My aunt Margaret often babysat Brian and Brenda and me when we were young. Margaret was older than my mother, and she suffered from mental retardation and hearing loss after having her tonsils become infected at the age of seven. Margaret, in her grown-up body, was stunted at the age of seven years old forever. She was the worst, bossiest seven-year-old that I ever knew. It was an awful age to be stuck at.

Margaret would always tattle on us when we did anything. She would run to Grandma and Mom, and she would twist her version of any story to make us look bad.

Margaret would read lips, and I would simulate curses at her with my mouth. She'd never heard curse words before her accident, so she would be trying to figure out the sounds that I was making with my mouth by repeating what they looked like. She could never figure out what I was trying to say, and I didn't care if she did know. I disliked her because she was so mean.

Besides everything else that was wrong with Margaret, she was epileptic too. I'd never seen her "pull a fit," as my mom would call it. But I knew I didn't want to be nearby when one happened.

Mom told me that they would have to put a wallet in her mouth to stop her from swallowing her tongue. It took many people to hold her down to prevent her from hurting herself.

If she didn't like me as much as I didn't like her, I imagined I would be in trouble if I were to be anywhere that she could get her hands on me during a fit.

I thought she must get all deformed and turn into a monster when it happened. Even though she never did touch me harshly, except to drag me by the arm to my mother or grandma with an accusation, I was afraid that in that "fit state" she might try to kill me.

She used to make sure I got reprimanded for taking a gingersnap cookie without asking, for moving a knickknack on a shelf, for not putting a dish in the sink or anything as lame as that.

Margaret and my grandma, Mom's mom, lived at the end of the street that I lived on. I could walk to visit Grandma anytime, and I used to love to be able to go to visit her all by myself. Margaret did not look pleased when I would show up without my mom to look after me. So I would do it often just to spite her.

One time I was about 15 and Margaret was at our house, and I had just asked Mom to teach me how to knit. My mom started a mitten for me and showed me how to knit, and I continued to knit by myself. Margaret saw me and said to my mom, "Annette, start me a mitt. I can knit too, better than her," she said, pointing at me.

So Mom started Margaret a mitt to knit too.

I was knitting away, and Margaret was knitting away too. She was sweating and mad because I was ahead of her.

"Stop," my mom yelled at me. "You're going to make Margaret take a fit, slow down!"

So I had to keep taking breaks so Margaret could catch up.

Grandma had a special little bottle of holy oil that had been blessed by the priest, and when I would get earaches from the wind or the water, she would dab a cotton ball with it and put it into my ear. The oil was magic. It always made my earaches disappear.

Grandma got married for the fourth time when she was 75. She married at the Catholic church in Nairn. A dinner and dance were held afterward at the Nairn Community Center. The Catholic Church didn't have to annul any of her marriages, because all three of her other husbands had died.

We always called her Grandma Badgerow. I don't imagine her new husband appreciated that much.

Her first husband had a bad heart and died of a heart attack. The second husband, who was my mom's dad, had developed cancer of the mouth. The cancer eventually took him away from Grandma too. Then Grandpa Badgerow was a lot older than Grandma, and he just died of old age.

Brian and Brenda knew Grandpa Badgerow. When they were little, he was still alive. He was gone before I came into the world. Now Grandma was marrying a new Grandpa, from French River.

Grandma was a religious woman. She always had lots of little fables and Bible stories to tell us about. No matter what you asked her, she'd have an answer for you. You could talk to her about anything and nothing surprised her. I loved her a lot.

Grandma Badgerow and the new Grandpa moved to French River after they were married. Margaret went with them.

We would occasionally go to French River to visit them. Grandma's homes always smelled like lilac or lavender; they were always old houses with lots of little rooms. There were funny little feather mattresses on the beds that we'd sleep on when we visited. I guess she kept all of the old homemade beds and mattresses that she used when all of her kids were at home.

My grandmother had a box of letters she had kept that were written to her by my mother's father. She gave them to my mother to keep and remember him by. They were letters telling Grandma what he was going through in his last days in the hospital.

They were love letters, I thought. He'd gone miles away to the hospital in Toronto. He found out he had cancer of the mouth and was getting treatment there. But with nine kids at home, Grandma could not go with him to help care for him.

My mother was five when her father died. She only remembers certain smells and feelings she had about him. She can't remember what he looked like or sounded like. I can't even imagine having been without her dad at such a young age.

The letters are quite touching. The last letter made me cry each time I would read it. It was a telegram from the hospital saying that Grandpa had died of cancer. Grandma never saw him again.

My mother has promised to leave the letters to me when she passes. I hope my children will enjoy them too.

There is also a very old book of remedies and medicine for ailments that was given to my mother from Grandma Badgerow. Mom used many of the concoctions out of that book to try to heal us when we were sick. Most of them were old wives' tales.

I remember one remedy in particular—a picky wool sock soaked in mustard and tied around your neck. It was awful and itchy and was supposed to help to rid you of a head cold. The pickiness and smell certainly made you stop thinking about the cold. It was dreadfully itchy to keep around your neck. I don't think it did anything for the cold, but it did make you stop complaining.

When we would go to weddings and events, my mom had a friend, Mrs. Merton, who could sew, and she would make me homemade dresses. The fabrics she and Mom chose, I thought, were so picky that I would not bend or turn for the entire time I'd have them on.

Mom would get angry at me because everyone could see how uncomfortable I was in the dresses. People would ask Mom, "What's wrong with Poochie?"

I would be standing there all stiff and not wanting to move and touch the seams on my underarms or waist. I really could not wait to take it off and get the scratchy seams, collar and waistband away from my skin.

Mom always seemed to pick the same material to put me in, too. She said it was a non-wrinkling material, and it always looked nice. Ick, I still hate polyester.

My father's mother was very prim and proper and cared a lot about the way things looked to people around her. She didn't seem to like the grandkids much. She'd complain whenever we were around.

Grandma Marcoux lived in Espanola, and we didn't visit her much. Her husband died before I was born too, so I never really knew him. She never remarried because she was afraid of what people would say about her if she did.

She was at my aunt Fern's House quite often when we went to visit. I guess Aunty Fern was one of her favourites.

Christmas would come, and Grandma Marcoux would give us kids all strange amounts of money, like $3.11. The amount was never an even number of money. I never ever understood what the point of the money was or why she even bothered giving it to us.

Grandma Badgerow, my mother's mother, would give us little soaps and bath things that she had found around her house. Some things were re-gifts.

Some of Grandma Badgerow's gifts were hand-knit socks or mitts made especially for us. Her gifts were always made with individual careful thought for each one of us.

Christmases were huge. One year we had a nice real balsam tree. We had to dispose of it even before Santa came. It turned out Mom was allergic to balsam.

Mom's lips got swelled up like two sausages on her face, just in time for Christmas that year. We hoped she wouldn't stay like that. It would be embarrassing to take her out to see people.

From then on, our tree was always an artificial one. Mom didn't like the needles all over the house that came from the real ones anyway, and she said they were dirty.

We had to get an artificial Christmas tree. With all of the lights and tinsel, the fake tree looked just as good as the real ones. It just didn't have the smell or the allergen factor. Artificial trees were a lot easier to put away when Christmas was over than the picky, sticky real ones too.

The gifts from Santa would show up while we were out visiting our relatives. They would be piled so high you couldn't see the Christmas tree behind them.

When my family got home and saw all of the presents under the tree, I would have to go and spend the rest of the evening in the bathroom holding my aching belly. I would become so tense with anticipation that I would get sick to my stomach.

When the clock would strike twelve, Dad would yell, "It's Christmas time! We can open our gifts." This was the way our traditional Christmas would be after Santa was no longer part of the event.

Miraculously, all the pain would subside, and I would be able to participate in the festivities with the waiting and anticipation finally done with.

Mom and Dad would let us open the gifts on Christmas Eve. That made it easier for them to enjoy the rest of the evening—knowing that we wouldn't be up and in their hair at the crack of dawn anxiously awaiting present-opening time. They could continue celebrating with beer and drinks and fun until the early morning hours.

We would stay up late on Christmas Eve until we were exhausted. The next day Dad would be hung-over, but he would still help us put things together or construct things that we had to build before we could play with them.

Chapter 40

GODPARENTS

I HAD A SPECIAL GODMOTHER—AUNTY Lilly, we called her, and her husband, my godfather, was Uncle Mel.

They tried to have children eight times. Aunty Lilly either had miscarriages or she had stillbirths or the babies died shortly after they were conceived or born.

One of their babies was born at the same time as I was and died shortly afterward from complications, my mom told me.

Uncle Mel and Aunty Lilly begged my mom and dad to let them have me. Mom said, "Dad and I couldn't just give up a baby that way!" So Uncle Mel and Aunty Lilly became my godparents. They would come over, and I would sit on Uncle Mel's knee for hours at the table with them while they talked with my parents. Uncle Mel would take me to the general store or to the gas station to buy things for me.

Uncle Mel and Aunty Lilly brought me a truckload of presents every year for Christmas. They gave me expensive things from expensive stores. My mom was always upset because although they would do this for me, they brought my brother and sister nothing. Mom didn't think it was fair. I think it made Brian and Brenda envy and hate me. I'm sure they thought I was very spoiled. I guess I was.

It was quite suddenly when we stopped seeing Aunty Lilly and Uncle Mel for a while. I'd heard different stories about different things, but nothing I believed. I missed them incredibly, and I couldn't believe they could just abandon me like that.

One day, Mom and Dad decided that we would go over to visit. I was 12 and it had been a while since we had seen them. It felt just like old times when we arrived there.

We were sitting at the kitchen table together and Mom mentioned that she thought I was like a crow, the way I liked to look at shiny things.

Aunty Lilly suggested I go into her and Uncle Mel's bedroom and get her jewellery box and look at her shiny jewellery. I suppose she suggested it to get my parents alone to talk.

I went to Aunty Lilly and Uncle Mel's bedroom and took the jewellery box off of the dresser. I sat down on their bed and opened it up. It was a treasure chest full of big beautiful shiny necklaces, bracelets, rings and brooches, all made of gold and silver and rhinestones. I thought I was in heaven. I had to try them all on and look at myself in the mirror.

The adults all seemed happy that I had found something to occupy myself with while they sat and chatted.

My uncle Mel, on his way past to the bathroom, came in and sat down beside me on the bed. He took my hand and held it. "You're what, twelve now? You're turning into a woman!" he said.

I was uncomfortable. Uncle Mel had a strange look in his eyes, like the coyote on Bugs Bunny.

"You'll soon be growing hair down there," he said, pointing to my vagina. "Is there any there yet?" he asked.

Maybe I was making too much of it, but I thought a grown man wasn't supposed to ask little girls questions of that sort. My dad would never ask me about something like that!

I felt dirty and disgusted with Uncle Mel. I pulled my hand out of his and rushed out of the room. I ran to Mom's side and didn't leave from there for the rest of the time that we visited.

Mom got terribly annoyed that I was being so clingy. "Go and play," she kept telling me. I did not listen to her. I was too afraid to get caught alone by Uncle Mel again. He had creeped me out.

On our way home that night, once we had left Uncle Mel and Aunty Lilly's house. Mom made sure I knew that she was upset with me for hanging off of her and not giving them any space while we were visiting. She said, "You know better than to hang around with the adults when we were talking." So I told her the words that Uncle Mel had said to me.

Mom yelled, "Oh my God, Rog, the damn stories about Mel are true, that son of a bitch!"

I didn't know what that meant, but my mom was pretty angry already and I thought questioning her might get her even angrier. I stayed quiet until we got home and then went straight to my room.

It was late when we got home. I had fallen asleep in the truck, and sometimes Mom would let me go to bed with no pyjamas on when that happened. It would be easier to put me into my bed and just cover me up than struggle with my sleepy limbs to try to get my pyjamas on.

I pleaded with her to let me sleep naked. Mom just looked at me and said straight out, "No, you can never sleep naked again!"

I put my flannelette pyjamas on quietly and got into my bed. *She is really angry with me*, I thought to myself.

I had really bad dreams about Uncle Mel that night. I never wanted to go see him or be alone with him again.

The next day I talked to Brenda about the incident. Brenda told me that she'd had a similar thing happen with Uncle Mel when she was about 12. When she told Mom and Dad, they did not really believe her. But that was why we stopped going there. Mom told Brenda that they certainly would not force her to go to Uncle Mel and Aunty Lilly's house again, and we would not invite them back over to ours.

I thought Brenda didn't like them because of all of the attention they gave me. I never knew why she didn't want to see them anymore. I never really understood until now.

I don't know if Mom and Dad talked to Uncle Mel and Aunty Lilly about it. We just never saw them again after that. There were no more phone calls, no more Christmas visits and Easter visits, not anything. No more gifts, no more hugs and kisses and no more godparents for me.

I thought that Uncle Mel must have a sickness to make him act and think so weird. I wondered why he thought about the things that he did. It was pretty gross and confusing to me.

I didn't want to see him anymore, and I felt ashamed about it. They had both loved me for so many years, and they had never been bad to me before. I don't know how Uncle Mel could have turned on me like that.

I felt that I still loved him, and I felt guilty. I would now abandon them, and they would be all alone. There would be no more children in their lives.

I used to think often about how they had wanted me at birth. I used to imagine the attention and love I would get if I had gone to live with them. If I had been their only child. I shivered thinking what my life might have been like with them now with this information.

I wondered if they missed me. I wondered if they were lonely. Aunty Lilly didn't deserve to be stuck with a man like Uncle Mel.

I thought to myself, *Everything must happen for a reason.*

Chapter 41

FROZEN IN THE ICE

WE WOULD GO TO OUR cottage in the winter riding on snow machines. We had two machines, and we had friends who Mom and Dad would take up with us.

We would cross the Nairn Dam on foot. Dad would carefully walk the machines across the dam because the path was narrow and dangerous.

Along the trails that led the way to the camp, we would stop on our machines every now and then so that the adults could all take a swig from the old wineskin that Dad would carry over his shoulder.

When we got to the cottage, we would go ice fishing and sliding, and Dad would shovel a big square of ice off on the lake to make a skating rink. One time, I remember skating all the way across the lake on smooth glare ice. The lake hadn't frozen until after the first snowfall. It was amazing to be able to skate all the way across. It felt like skating on the most enormous skating rink in the world.

It was beautiful; the ice just went on forever. It wasn't much good for snowmobiles, though. It was much too slippery.

In the winter of 1975, while we were at the camp, the weather had become mild, and the lake had turned to slush. It was too deep to drive the snow machines through.

Jim and Carol, the other couple, and Mom and Dad and I stayed in the camp all day and played Pass the Ace or Rumoli, card games Mom and Dad always played with their friends. We played cards for quarters and nickels for hours together by the heat of the woodstove.

Mom and Dad and their friends drank all day and were "feeling no pain," as my father would put it. We saw lights across the lake around ten p.m. while we were sitting at the table playing cards, but we thought nothing of it.

We were ready to go to bed around one o'clock. My father opened the patio doors to get a bit of air and have a pee off of the balcony. We could hear a faint screaming of "help." The yelling was coming from somewhere on the ice, far off into the dark cold distance.

Everybody who was in our camp went out to the patio to listen. We concluded that it had to have been the snow-machine lights that we'd witnessed earlier. Somebody must have attempted to cross the lake through the slush and gotten the snow machines stuck. We were worried—the lights that we'd seen on the lake, we'd seen quite a few hours ago.

My father and Jim had to get themselves geared up pretty good to walk out through the icy water. Dad had hip waders, and he gave them to Jim to put on over his winter boots. Mom tucked the felts from my Dad's boots into green Glad garbage bags, and Dad put them back into his snow boots. My Dad and Jim took flashlights, and they set out to find the people on the ice.

We were afraid of how much time the people had been out there. We thought that they might be close to freezing to death.

Dad decided that he and Jim should take a snow machine to get out as far as possible, so they could get to the people fast and get them out of the cold. The machines were not a concern at that point.

We saw the lights of our snow machine go down into the slush when Dad and Jim slowed down. Then Mom, Carol and I were afraid for Dad and Jim getting stranded as well. Finally we could hear Dad yelling, "Everything is okay," and we could see their waving flashlights, trying to assure us that they were all right.

It was a while still before a survivor would finally make it to our camp from out of the slush. A man stumbled up to our camp. Each of his boots had frozen ice stuck in huge chunks all the way around his feet.

He had to struggle to lift his feet to walk because they had become so heavy. He was exhausted, and he no longer had feeling in his feet or hands.

He informed us that he saw my father and his friend out on the lake. He had helped Dad and Jim as much as he could to find the two other people. Dad told him to just try to save himself. He instructed the man to walk to our camp to safety; he and Jim would continue the search for the other couple.

The man said that he and the other couple had gotten separated when they hit the water. They saw our camp lights and started walking toward them for help. This lonely survivor just figured that his companions would be walking toward the same lights that he saw. Our camp lights were the only ones on the lake.

When the lights had started to dim because we were getting ready for bed, the bunch of them were terrified of getting disoriented and losing their way. That was when they started yelling to us for help. Lucky for them, my dad needed to relieve his bladder and chose to do it on the front balcony. Leaving the door open allowed us all at the camp to hear their screaming.

The cold man knew he could still make it on his own when he left Dad and Jim in the dark, on the ice, to search for the others. So he left to save himself. He was feeling guilty.

We took the man into the camp, and he took off all of his clothes. Mom gave him warm blankets and coffee and sat him near the fire. We tried to help him warm up and to make him comfortable.

We sat still and kept quiet, in the camp, looking out into the darkness for any sign of my Dad or Jim's flashlight. Dad and Jim looked for a long period, leaving us all afraid for their lives as well.

Suddenly, we heard Dad yell, "We found them!" We were so relieved to hear him.

It was still a while before Dad and Jim returned to our cottage. Miraculously, they got themselves and the couple back to us. My dad and Jim were carrying the others as they tried to walk alongside.

With as much physical energy as they could muster, the couple helped themselves through the icy water, leaning on Dad and Jim. The whole bunch of them were cold or frozen and exhausted.

The woman walked in with bare feet. She collapsed into our arms in the camp. She had taken off her boots and put her feet in her husband's Ski-Doo suit to keep her warm. Her boots had gotten too heavy for her to drag through the ice. She had lost hope when the lights that they were walking toward had started to dim.

They informed us that they had stopped trudging through the ice together and lay down and were preparing to die. They told us that their snow machines had sunk into the slushy water on the other side of the lake. The only thing they could see was our cottage lights in the distance.

They were so relieved to have something to guide them toward safety. They had not, however, been able to judge the distance and the time it was going to take them to get to us.

The lady's feet were a greyish blue, and all of the survivors' hands were the same shade. Their clothes were frozen onto them. Their zippers were almost impossible to unzip.

Dad said it was lucky that he and Jim found the couple when they did. The warm spell from the day before that had turned everything to slush was starting to break. It was getting colder, and things were beginning to freeze again. We would have found them the next day, frozen into the lake.

We warmed the strangers by the woodstove, wrapped them in blankets and gave them coffee or alcohol or whatever they wanted to get them warm and comfortable. The couple was so happy to see their friend was alive and there with us already. They all broke into tears of joy to see one another alive.

Dad took the snow machine that we had left at the camp. He drove to the nearest place where he knew there was a telephone to get in touch with help. He called the police and an ambulance from Espanola and returned to us.

The roads to the cottage were not ploughed in the winter. With the one snow machine and a toboggan, Dad would have to find a way to get the survivors 20 miles down the road to where the ambulance would be waiting for them.

My father strapped the man and his wife on the toboggan. The third man rode on the back of the machine with Dad. They would snow-machine to the end of the trail where it met up with the highway. Help would be waiting for them there.

We were afraid to let them go. If anything happened to the last machine, they could be stranded again. We did know that the Espanola police would be waiting for them, and if they did not show up, the police would have a search sent out. Even if the drop-off went according to plan, my dad would have to come back alone, and that worried us.

Dad returned within two hours, and he was sight for sore eyes. Everything had miraculously worked out for the best. The ambulance was there to meet them at the road as soon as Dad got there. My dad helped the people into the ambulance, hugged them all with heartfelt good-byes and wished them the best of luck. He watched the lights of the ambulance taking them away as he left to head back to all of us at the camp who were waiting to have him back safely.

That night, nobody could even imagine going to bed and trying to go to sleep. The energy level in the camp was so high that we were wound up like toy soldiers, remembering the details and reliving the incident for hours.

All the snow machines that went down that night were under ice in the morning. We went out to look for them and realized they would have to be chipped and dug out.

We spoke to many people about that night's event. We were told that putting the frozen people near the fire and allowing them any alcohol was not the right thing to have done. They should have been warmed up slowly. We should not have given them alcohol. Alcohol slows the blood circulation and promotes the loss of blood to the extremities.

If we'd known the proper care for rescuing frozen people, we surely would have given it. We did the best that we could do. They were very grateful and happy to have their lives saved by any means.

We felt bad for not knowing the things we should have done, but if it ever happened again, we would be much better prepared for knowing the information.

The three survivors came to visit us in the summer. They told us over and over again how grateful they were and that we had saved their lives. They thanked us and brought us gifts, and they reassured us that our help was so appreciated and that they would have done the same things for anyone who had been in that situation.

We were overjoyed to see them again to find out how everything turned out for them.

They said that when their hands and feet thawed out, there was great pain from the areas that had gotten frostbitten. The lady had lost some toes due to frostbite, but they were so very happy and grateful to be alive.

Mom wrote a letter to Glad, the garbage-bag company, that spring. She wanted to thank them for making such strong garbage bags. Mom told the Glad people of our experience using their garbage bags to keep Dad's feet dry and how they helped us to save lives on the lake that night.

Glad, in return, sent us about a year's supply of garbage bags to show their appreciation to us for sharing our story with them.

Chapter 42

POURING AT NIAGARA

*H*IGH SCHOOL WAS ANOTHER DRAMATIC time for me; another big change in my life was going to take place. I knew it was coming, just as I'd known public school was coming nine years before.

I'd have to get up early in the morning to catch the school bus to Espanola. I would be going 20 minutes away to get to school. I would be unable to get home if I got sick, and I would be stranded there for each entire day. Knowing that I could not run home if I needed to really bothered me.

My anxiety all started in the summer of the year leading up to high school in 1975, when I was 13. My family took a camping trip to Niagara Falls. We took my mom's sister Ann and her husband, Norm, and their three boys with us on this trip. The adults stayed in a campground in our camper, and the kids slept in our sleeping bags in the back of my dad's truck, which had a box on it for shelter from mosquitoes or rain.

My cousins and I traveled from Nairn to Niagara Falls in the back of the truck. We were happy to arrive at the campsite. We swam in the pool and enjoyed the sunshine. We looked forward to seeing Marineland and all of the sights the Niagara area entailed.

The second day we were at the campground, we had a big lunch of sandwiches and corn on the cob, which I loved. Then we locked up the trailer up and drove to Marineland to spend the day.

We hadn't been there an hour when my stomach started cramping up. I had to look for a bathroom quickly. My mom came with me, and we found the lady's public washroom.

There was a line of about 20 ladies ahead of me. I started to panic and almost passed out from cramps. Suddenly, I had no choice but to let go or die right there on the spot. I filled my pants while I stood in the line.

The fact that I had white crop pants on and had just filled them with diarrhea was so embarrassing. I had to tell my mom, and she stood behind me to save me the humiliation of being seen like that.

I finally got into a stall, and diarrhea just poured out of me. "Just go," I told Mom, "just leave me here!" I cried. I did not want to leave the bathroom with my pants the way they were, and I thought I could stay there in that stall for the rest of the day and hide.

My mom stood outside the bathroom door, telling me, "Poochie, you will be okay, just relax and I will be right out here for you!"

The sweat was pouring off of my face, and my pants were a disgusting mess.

I didn't know how I was going to get out of the bathroom and escape the humiliation. My mom told me to give her my pants, so I did. She went to the sink and washed them out with soap and water until they were clean.

Other women kept coming and going around us.

Finally, the wave of cramping and heaving ended, and the sweat and diarrhea stopped pouring out of me. I was shaking and crying, and the whole thing was so terrible. I didn't know how I was going to get through the park without everyone laughing and pointing at me.

I waited in the stall and Mom returned with a wad of wet paper towels. "Use this to clean yourself up," she said and handed it to me under the door. I used the wet towel and wiped myself clean. I just wanted to somehow get to the truck, lie down and be alone.

Mom handed me my pants under the stall door. They were white again. I was so amazed, so relieved, to get them back clean. I felt the fear subside.

Maybe I could get out of this after all and escape the terrible scene and embarrassment that I had envisioned myself having to go through. I prayed.

Mom quietly said to me, through the door, "Put your pants back on. They will dry. I will give you my sweater to tie around your waist."

I put the pants on. I took Mom's sweater, which she handed me from under the stall door, and tied it around my waist.

It was very hot outside; I knew that being cold in the wet pants would not be an issue.

The pants were a pale transparent white when they were wet, and even if they were see-through, at least they were clean and would dry. With the sweater over them, no one could really tell that anything had happened.

I came out of the stall and gave Mom a very relieved and grateful smile. She took me to the sink and helped me to wash off my face and comb my hair. The sweat and tears had the upper half of me looking like a mess too.

Mom hugged me and said, "Don't worry, we will not go too far from a bathroom. If it happens again, we will just do the same thing again. You are not alone," she comforted me. "I am here to help you."

Mom and I walked out of the bathroom and she said, "No one has to know anything!"

I felt such relief and so thankful to her. I was not even going to have to tell the others what had happened. I felt like she had just saved my life.

The day went on, and I never had to return to the bathroom. The fear of having to go never left me, but occasionally I would forget and enjoy myself. No one knew anything had happened but Mom and me.

We discovered later that whenever I attempted to eat corn, the same stomach problems would occur. I had developed an allergy to it. I couldn't go an hour after eating it, and I was in the bathroom with it pouring right out of me. It would be tough to give up corn.

I did love it, but it didn't like me, and I wasn't going to let that happen to me again.

Fearful of having something take control of me without warning and cause me that distress again, I never wanted to go anywhere that I couldn't get to a bathroom quickly or didn't have Mom nearby to save me.

High school was the next step in my life. I had so much anxiety about going. Mom would not be there if anything happened, and what if I couldn't get to the bathroom in time again? A phobia was born.

Chapter 43

GAINING CONTROL

*I*N GRADE 9, I SPENT much of the year in the bathroom cramped and nauseated, throwing up, feeling very ill and wanting to go home without being able to leave. I just had to think about the cramps and they would happen. I'd have to call Mom to come and get me.

My mom would drive to the school and pick me up and bring me home. She felt helpless. She brought me to the doctors to find out what the problem was.

I would wake up at night and go lay on the couch in the living room crying with cramps, and now I was also developing shooting pains through my chest. Mom brought me back to the doctor. He checked and did all kinds of tests and X-rays and ultrasounds. He was trying to figure out what these terrible stomach problems and chest pains were.

I was diagnosed with gallstones, which showed up on an X-ray. The doctors showed my mom and me the X-ray and explained to us what gallstones were and what could be done about them. This explanation made my mother feel better. Now she had something to work with. She cut out fried foods and fatty foods from my diet, which was just about all I ever ate. With the fat removed from my diet, I stopped suffering the shooting pains through the chest.

I still did not believe that because these gallstones were under control that I would be alright. My thought process had a lot to do with the stomach problems, but I didn't know that at the time.

Mom and the doctors came to another prognosis. They believed that it was some sort of anxiety that I was suffering with. "Your nerves are causing the pains," I was told. I thought they would have to operate and take my nerves out or something. They didn't. They just sent me home to suffer.

Mom would tell me to get busy while I was at school, listen and do well on my school work, and I would be all right. She asked, "What is the worst thing that could happen to you?"

"I would have to go to the bathroom and not be able to make it there. I would make a mess of myself, have to stay at school all day, and go home on the bus with all of the other kids laughing at me. Then I would have to go back the next day and the next," I answered her in tears.

Mom said she had a solution. She sent me to school again, but with a note telling the teaching staff to allow me to leave the classroom to go to the bathroom whenever I needed, without having to ask permission. She told them I had stomach problems, so this was necessary.

I went back to school the next day and handed the note to the principal. He did not ask any questions, he just told me not to worry. He would tell each of my teachers to allow me that freedom.

I felt slightly ill on occasion but would just excuse myself and go to the bathroom. By the time I would get to the bathroom, the feeling would be gone. I took advantage of the opportunity about three more times, and then the fear and anxiety subsided.

The routine became normal for me to just get up and go to school in the morning. I felt safe knowing that I could take control of myself when and if stomach cramps suddenly tried to take me over again. I could keep one step ahead of them and be sure to make it to the bathroom if I needed to, without being denied.

My fear had been in the loss of control and being held back. The phobia was developed by being stranded with no control and having to wait in line to relieve myself. Now that the obstacles were gone, I was safe and back in charge. My mind stopped trying to fool me into believing that I was ill and alone and had no place to go for relief.

On occasion, when I was anyplace and did not see a bathroom or know where there was one, immediately my phobia would come back. I would become anxious and start to feel ill. I would not settle down until I found the restroom, and then I would be fine.

Chapter 44

BILLY

MY MOTHER'S SISTER ANN WAS married to a man named Norm, who was at least 11 years older than her. He always seemed like a very old man to me, but they were happy together.

I remember Aunty Ann and Uncle Norm smoking all the time. Mom not did like to go there to visit after she had finally, really quit smoking. Dad had not smoked for years, and when he quit, he just got up and decided that he'd had enough of it and never looked back. It never bothered him a bit if someone else smoked around him or not.

Now that Mom had been away from smoking for a while, she would tell people that she missed it. I hated hearing her say that. It scared me. I felt that she still wanted to smoke. I was afraid because of all the cancer hype from cigarette smoking and the deaths we had started learning about that were associated with smoking. I didn't worry about Dad—when he was done with something, he was done.

I spent lots of time at my aunt Ann's in my early teen years. I would get off the school bus at my cousin Billy's house to spend the weekends. I guess I'd just gotten used to the smoke when I was there. I'd stop noticing it after I'd be there for awhile.

Billy had two younger brothers, Michael and a little pest named Robbie. Michael was quiet and really kept to himself. Robbie was loud and always swearing and saying rude things. I thought Robbie was going to be a badass from the moment I laid eyes on him.

Around my house, cursing was something you didn't even think of doing in front of my mom and dad. Dad could do it, because it was the way the men at the mine would talk and it was hard for him to quit. If Dad caught us swearing—well, Brian really—he would slap him on the head with his huge index finger. Brian would walk away with his mouth shut and a sore head.

Dad's finger always scared us kids out of swearing; when he'd flick it on your head like that, it hurt real bad.

One time long ago, Brian was sitting and watching TV with Aunty Lilly. He had a quick, unaware tendency to use bad words a lot whenever he spoke. All the adults were trying to curb him of his bad habit. While watching TV, he got excited and said "cocksu . . . ," but he stopped himself and looked back at Aunty Lilly.

"Gee," Brian said, "I almost said *cocksucker*, aye, Aunty Lilly?"

Aunty Lilly laughed and said, "Almost, aye Brian!" She told everybody this story afterward. Brian really had a foul mouth from listening and trying to be like Dad too much, I guess. Eventually, Brian was able to stop himself before the swear word came out, but not without a lot of the reprimanding by Dad's big finger on the top of his head.

Billy was like a brother to me. He and I would spend nights sitting up on the pull-out couch where I would sleep when I was there. Billy would talk about his thoughts on girls, and I talked about my thoughts on boys. We would correct or explain to each other little things about the opposite sex. I would ask him all the personal things that there were to know about boys. He would ask me all the personal stuff that he wanted to know about girls.

Billy was as afraid as I was to have anything to do with sex with anybody at that time. We were young and both very immature. We thought that having sex meant you were in your last and most important relationship and you were ready to marry.

We got along so well, I think, because we were both in the same stages of our youth at the same time.

I met Billy's friend and neighbour Alan. The three of us often went tobogganing in the back hills of McKerrow, where they both lived. Alan was funny and sweet, and I really liked him. I wanted to go to Billy's house on the weekends even more often after I met Al.

Billy and I would spend a lot of time at Alan's house. Alan's parents had a finished basement and a record player where we would end up dancing to music. More often, it was me dancing slow songs with Alan, and Billy playing air-hockey alone.

Billy, Michael, Robbie, Alan and I, along with Alan's sisters and brother, would go Ski-Doo-ing and sliding, and spend hours and hours together behind McKerrow. We'd have fires near the hills to keep warm and cook hot dogs and beans for lunch.

Alan always treated me like a princess, helping me with my coat and opening the door for me. I never dated Alan because he was 13, too young for me. I was 14. I was going to be in high school the following year, and that would not have looked good. I was worried about what everybody else might think. I must have inherited that way of thinking from Grandma Marcoux, because usually I didn't care what anyone thought. But it was in my head that if anyone saw me with Alan, they would think I was immature.

Alan and Billy and I stayed close friends on the weekends only. I always came back to Alan, in my mind, when I envisioned the perfect boyfriend.

Billy loved to snowmobile, and one year while he was out Ski-Doo-ing around, he missed seeing the clothesline in the yard, ran directly into it and nearly hung himself by his mouth. He broke some teeth and was pretty lucky to have come away with his head still on his shoulders that day.

Alan's father died in a snowmobile accident that year. He drove right over the edge of a cliff that he did not see for the snow. I felt sorry for Alan having to go through that. I'm sure it was the most difficult thing that anyone could have to live through, losing a parent!

Billy started working, helping a 35-year-old woman at the end of the street where he lived by doing chores for her. Billy was in Grade 10. He spent lots of time with her; she seduced him when he was 15, and he never left her side afterward.

They moved into her house together. I thought he was crazy getting involved with someone so old. His mom would not let him back into the house unless he stopped seeing her. I never understood how Aunty Ann of all people could condemn Billy for getting involved with someone older, when she had done the same thing by marrying a man 11 years her elder.

Billy did not put an end to his relationship with the woman to come back and be with his family. We had already stopped hanging around so much when he started to help the woman; his weekends would be tied up. I never really ever got to see him again as a teenager after that.

I lost touch with Billy, and I only would see Alan at high school once he finally started.

My Uncle Norm and Aunty Ann were not very happy. They stopped talking or visiting everyone because they were embarrassed about Billy leaving them for the old lady. Mom and Dad and I would often see Aunty Ann and Uncle Norm at the mall, getting groceries. They would usually pretend they did not see us.

I think Aunty Ann was very sad and thought she had somehow failed as a mother. We never felt that way about her. We loved her, and Mom would always call her and stop by her house to see her on her way into Espanola. Aunty Ann would not answer the phone, and she would pretend she was not at her house when we visited. She would hide inside and not answer the door.

Aunty Ann used to be fun and outgoing, and now she was like a ghost, lurking somewhere behind the scenes. Her life was changed drastically by Billy's actions.

Chapter 45

GRADE 9

ᕼIGH SCHOOL HAD BECOME A safe haven in Grade 10 in 1976. I started to confidently get on with my life. When I was used to school and resigned to all of its qualities, I was drawn to art, architectural drafting and English.

I hated math with a passion. My mom would try, with much difficulty, to help me understand it. But I ended up failing it the first year. I finally achieved my Grade 9 math credit when I was in Grade 10 and my Grade 10 math credit in Grade 11. I only needed two credits in math for my Grade 12 diploma, and once I had both of them I never took math again. I was very fortunate to have had my mom help me do the math homework.

With Mom's help, I could achieve a decent grade. I would just need to get myself over the exemption mark in class to avoid having to write the exams. I'd still write the exams, but my exam marks alone would never have gotten me a math credit.

My problem with math was, I'd no sooner start to understand one procedure than we'd go on to learn something else. As soon as I understood the next thing, I'd forget the first one I'd learned. Passing an exam would have been out of the question.

I didn't take gym after the first year either. I hated taking my clothes off in front of other girls. I felt like they were laughing at me. I had one breast half-developed and the other breast not even starting. I had to wear my big-ass granny panties, which no one else wore anymore, and I thought I would be a laughingstock. Plus I hated physical education. I couldn't find a purpose for it in my life.

I loved art, drawing and creating things from my imagination. I enjoyed drawing fantasy worlds and cartoon characters. I did well in art until Grade 11, when I had a new art teacher. He told me he did not want me to draw things that were not real anymore. He wanted to see me do drawings of still-life things. He'd always mark my work with 9 out of 10 and 9.5 out of 10.

Another girl in my class did really well in art. All she did was reproduce other people's work. To a tee, mind you, but to me that was cheating. She'd have drawings reproduced that Robert Bateman had done and other well-known artists. They were really great forgeries.

She would never do anything original, but the teacher never complained about her art. He felt she could draw things she saw, and that took the skill he was looking for. The "copier," I'll call her, and I competed in art class all through high school for 10 out of 10s on our work.

The copier would always get 10 out of 10 on her reproductions, and I would get 9 out of 10 on my imagination drawings. I was sure that the teacher just didn't like me and gave her the extra mark just to spite me.

I gave in, and I drew the teacher a picture of the barn next door to my house. I got a mark of 10 out of 10. Drawing real things was boring and not much of a challenge. However, just for the marks, I continued to draw stuff around the house for him for the rest of the year.

The copier and I, at the end of the Grade 11, spring semester, were both asked if we would allow the school to put some of our artwork into a gallery exhibit at the Espanola Mall. I chose my imagination drawings, and she had her reproductions. People were impressed by both of our exhibits. I realized that in the art world, there were many different styles of artist, each style having its own following of appreciative admirers.

I was honoured to have been offered the privilege of having my artwork displayed on behalf of Espanola High School for all of the surrounding area's people to view. It was a real boost to my confidence to see the people walking by the exhibits and spending so much time looking at and enjoying my creations.

Chapter 46

UNDER WHERE

I CAME HOME FROM SCHOOL with a spot of blood in my panties. I showed my mom because I didn't know if this was it, the dreaded period, or not. She looked at me and said, "That's your period, you've started!" I was so relieved and overjoyed to finally have turned into a woman with my other women friends.

Mom bought me pads. I had to have a belt on to attach them to. The belt went around your waist and had a clip in the front and one in the back. The clips held the pad in place to prevent it from moving and sliding down your leg. I hated the whole contraption. I felt like everybody must know when I had one in my pants. It was so big and bulky.

I begged Mom to get me some tampons. I told her that the other girls were using them. She argued with me a bit about tampons not being a morally appropriate way to contain my period. She did not think I should stick things up into myself at such a young age.

I convinced her of just how much easier it would be to contain my secret time of the month. I reminded her that tampons were used by all the girls my age nowadays. She gave in to the modern way of society and bought me a box.

I had the box of tampons ready for when the next period came. It started, and I struggled to get the tampon in. I didn't think my vagina could take it. When it finally went in, I didn't know how far to push it. I was afraid of losing it in there. I must have wasted 10 tampons before I felt confident enough to wear one.

If I walked out of the bathroom with one in, I had to know I wouldn't accidentally swallow it up or lose it through my pant leg without knowing it. The first time I wore one to school, I was in the bathroom half of the day checking to see that it was still there. I didn't want to lose it in any which way.

It wasn't very long before I got used to having the period come and go. I would get cramps every month, and I stopped being so excited about it.

Wearing the tampons was much better than the pads. I felt better concealed. I could even go swimming with one in and still not lose it. The tampons were a hit and proved to be quite an advantage for me to have fought for in the long run.

I also started to get breasts. Not much of them, but enough that I couldn't just wear my T-shirts anymore because it was obvious that I had nipples. They started to hurt when they would get cold and rub on my blouses or shirts. They would feel like chapped lips.

Mom took me out and bought me a training bra. *Oh my God*, I thought. *I hate this thing.* I felt like I was in a straightjacket. It reminded me of all the polyester dresses Mom used to make me wear. I told Mom, "I can't bear it!"

She said, "Well, you're going to have to get used to it."

"I can't," I cried. "It's awful!"

She just looked at me like I had two heads and said, "Well, what are you going to do?" Mom knew me by now, and there was no sense in trying to force me to wear it.

"I don't know," I said, "but I will think of something."

I had a nylon halter top that tied at the neck, and that became my new bra. It hid what it had to, and nobody knew any different, except for the little ties showing at the back of my neck sometimes. Mom would have to make sure it got in the wash every Wednesday. She knew I would be lost without it. It was the only one I had with double thickness to hide my nipples.

I remember Mom and all my girlfriends asking me when I was going to start to wear a real bra. I thought maybe I would never wear a real bra with all that yucky elastic in it. My friends teased me and then got used to seeing me in my halter top and left me alone about it.

Eventually, I started to become self-conscious about my friends finding out that I still didn't wear one. Mom bought me a few different types of bras to try to encourage me to wear one. I would wear them to school and run home to take them off as soon as I could. I thought about the discomfort every minute of every hour of every day whenever I had one on.

I realized, once again, that I just had to make myself do the right thing. I had to force myself to wear the bra. Somewhere along the way, I stopped thinking about it so much and, coincidentally, stopped having to take it off as soon as I got home.

I still hate bras. I don't know who invented them, but it had to have been someone who never had to wear one.

Chapter 47

NEW FRIENDS

I MET MICHELLE AT A dance in Nairn. We were both in Grade 10, and she was an Espanola girl. She'd come to Nairn just for the dance that was being held at the Nairn Community Center. I met her at the dance. She was there with a boy from Nairn who had apparently left her at the dance for another girl. I saw her sitting all alone and went to rescue her. She and I hit it off, and she ended up coming home to my house from the dance to stay for the weekend.

On our way home, when the dance was over, the girl who spent the evening with Michelle's date followed us along the road and taunted Michelle with words. Then she took a punch at Michelle and hit her in the eye. I came between them and stopped it from getting any worse. I don't know where I got the guts to do that, but I did.

I told the girl to leave Michelle alone or she'd be dealing with both of us. She looked at me and realized that I meant what I said. She turned and walked the other way. Michelle was so thankful, and I was so relieved. That girl was one of the badass kids in town who was always into trouble. We were lucky that I somehow got tough that night.

I was never a bully, never felt like it was a really great way to make good friends. But I was happy to be there for Michelle. With her I felt strength I would never have had alone.

Michelle ended up wearing glasses from the punch to the eye she received that night.

We became really good friends, and we were inseparable. We spent every spare minute, lunch hour and weekend together. My mom and dad liked her as much as I did. She was a great friend to me and my family. My dad's pet name for her was "Dummy." My dad thought she was pretty funny.

Michelle was sarcastic and sharp and challenged my wits. People would think we hated each other with the way that we communicated so sarcastically. It was just our way of being honest with each other. In our minds, it was constructive criticism, and it worked for us.

In school the next year, Grade 10, I met Nicky. She'd invite me for the weekend to stay with her at her parents' motel.

Nicky and Michelle did not get along very well. Michelle was a little too tomboyish for Nicky, and Nicky was too much of a girly-girl for Michelle. They didn't like each other's ways. I liked both of them, and I would rotate spending weekends with them.

Being able to have me for company only half the time wasn't a real hit with Michelle, but there was no getting her to hang out with Nicky, and I was not going to give Nicky up. I liked Nicky because she was girly and feminine. Femininity was becoming a quality that I admired and wanted to take on for myself. However, Michelle wanted to be just the opposite. I enjoyed being a hardass with Michelle, and I took my femininity lessons from Nicky every second weekend.

Nicky was adopted, which I found totally interesting. Her adoptive parents owned and ran the motel in Webwood. I asked Nick about her real mom. She said she was a baby when her mom had given her away. She said that one day she would try to find her, but she couldn't really do that until she was 18. It had something to do with the legal system. Also, she didn't want her adoptive parents to feel like she did not love them. Nicky felt that by looking for her real mom, she would be insulting her adoptive parents.

I just could not imagine her mother giving her up. Mothers were supposed to love and cherish their children like mine did.

We could eat whatever we wanted for dinner at Nicky's parents' motel restaurant when it was not too busy. When it was busy and they needed Nicky to work, I would help out by busing tables—bringing water to customers and cleaning the table when people were done eating.

Nicky was mature. She had boobs, a stunning figure and lots of really fashionable clothes. She had a boyfriend named Dale who lived in Sudbury, the big city 50 minutes from us.

She and Dale were together on some weekends. When she was not with him, she'd always be on the phone with him. She told me that they both hadn't had sex yet. She enjoyed my eager interest as she told me everything else that they did do together.

She was one of the prettiest girls in school and definitely one of the smartest. I looked up to her. My feelings for Nicky were part of why Michelle didn't really like her. Michelle never worried about her looks or her manners, and she was a downright crazy dresser and a lot of fun to be with.

Nicky's boyfriend would come to our high school to pick her up sometimes after school because he could drive. His parents didn't mind lending him their car. Nicky would make sure to walk by me and her other girlfriends at our lockers when she was with Dale, just to show him off. Sometimes, he would be wearing a Sudbury football jersey. We were so jealous of her. She had an awesome boyfriend from a different school, he was tall and handsome, and he was on a football team. Sometimes during the week, she would show up at school wearing his football jersey herself.

One night Nicky called me in tears. She told me that she and Dale had just spoken on the phone and split up. She wasn't really crying or depressed, she just wanted me to come over the next weekend because she wanted someone to talk to about it.

I went to her house the following weekend, and we spent the weekend together without the phone calls from Dale interrupting us every 10 minutes. She played the piano and we sang together. We took walks and looked for four-leaf clovers.

She talked about how she was really relieved that she and Dale broken up. He was getting too serious for her, and he wanted more from her than a friendship—meaning sex. Nicky told me she was not ready for sex. I understood how she felt. I agreed then that Dale was not good for her right now. We also agreed together that it was a good thing for her to try to forget about him.

It really didn't take that long for her to get over Dale, since he did not go to our school and she didn't have to see him every day.

We had a bunch of girls from school who hung around together. At the high-school dances and on our breaks and lunches, we'd be together. Finally, Michelle and Nicky got to know each other a little better and were okay with each other's company. I guess Michelle started to get in touch with her feminine side. It sure wasn't Nicky learning how to be butch.

There were a few other girls who were in different classes with each of us who hung out together as well. Michelle and Nicky and I and the others decided to plan a girl's trip up to my cottage one weekend. I passed the idea by Mom and she said it would be fun for us, as long as I cleaned it up the same way as I got it. "There's to be no drinking and no boys," she made sure to establish with me.

Mom knew she could trust her things with me. After all, I cleaned up at home for her sometimes. She was always happy with my work. Brian and Brenda were never allowed to use the camp alone. They would have parties at home when Mom and Dad were gone for the weekends. The place would be dirty when Mom and Dad got home, and nothing would be as Mom had left it. There was always something broken.

Mom had chrome chairs with booties she'd knit out of Fentex on them, to stop the floor from getting scratched. The chair by the wall behind the table had one bootie missing. If that chair was out of place when they got home, Mom knew that Brian or Brenda had to have had more than six friends over, because they needed to use the chair from the back of the table.

Brian and Brenda never caught on to Mom's trick. If they'd have known when they cleaned up after the party was over to put that same chair behind the table, they would have been scot-free.

All the girlfriends came to my place after school on the Nairn school bus on Friday. My Dad drove us up to our cottage to party. We sat in the back of the truck all the way from the highway, down the dusty camp road, singing and laughing, hanging from the tailgate.

Of course, one of the girls had a bottle of booze that she'd brought with her.

I started to cook dinner with everyone's help in the kitchen. I went into the oven drawer on the propane stove that was turned on. I grabbed a cast-iron frying pan and dropped it because it had scorched the whole inside of my hand. Gas-oven drawers got hot inside, not like electric stoves. A lesson well-learned. It was very painful. I held my hand under the tap with cold running water. I graduated to a coffee can full of cold water, which I carried around with my hand in to stop the burning for the rest of the evening. I was getting some relief from the stinging of the burn through the coolness of the water.

I got up to go get something, and when I returned, the girls were sitting at the table and looking at me strangely. I sat down and hurriedly put my hand back into the can. The girls all burst out laughing. They had put grease and butter and jam and all kinds of gunk into the can with my water. I didn't even look in the can before I stuck my hand in it.

Right after dinner, we started drinking the bottle of booze that one of the girls had smuggled up. The alcohol numbed the pain of the burn, and I even got my hand out of the can somehow.

We pulled pranks on each other all weekend and never knew when anyone was being serious. We were all "feeling no pain" from the liquor in our systems. We were laughing and crying and stumbling all over, it was a hoot!

The neighbour's son, Donald, and about 10 or 12 boys showed up next door. Donald had planned a guy's party at his cottage the same weekend. *How convenient*, I thought. I'm sure he knew I was having the girls up this weekend. Everybody on the bus home from school was talking about it.

I'm sure he figured he'd have the girls around anxiously wanting to join them, without even having to invite us to his party. I thought, *Men and their controlling behaviour, gotta love 'em!*

However, my love affair with Donald was over in grade school. There was no way this idea was going to pan out for him. The girls all made a pact, without my even having to say anything, to not to get involved with the boys next door. The girls all felt the same way as I did: this was a girls only weekend retreat. The boys did try to lure us over there and get us to join them, but my girls were strong, and we kept our word.

We all got drunk on our own. We'd walk the beach, teasing the boys and pretending that we were planning to go skinny-dipping later. I'm sure they were not pleased about Donald's lame party. We stuck it out. "No boys allowed!"

When we woke up in the morning, there was a boy in our cottage sleeping in the living-room armchair. None of us had any idea who he was or how or when he'd come into our camp. Wasn't the door locked when we went to bed? Who unlocked the door to let him in? Nobody was going to give in and tell; it was a mystery. "Sleeping beauty," we laughed as we shook him to wake him up. He woke up and laid there looking up at us like he was Goldilocks.

He didn't know how he'd got into our camp either. He was drunk when he came in, in the middle of the night, and he thought that he was at Donald's camp. This guy just figured that everyone in Donald's camp had gone to bed, so he fell asleep in the chair.

The next thing we knew, there were police officers at my back door saying that they were looking for this kid. He'd run away from home, apparently, because he wasn't allowed to go to Donald's party. When he was gone for two days, his parents called the police.

The kid had told Donald about running away from home. Donald kicked him out of his camp during the night. He didn't want to be harbouring a fugitive.

Lucky for us, all of our booze was gone, and we had sobered up. We were not old enough to be drinking, and we were very fortunate that the policemen hadn't shown up the night before.

The cops took the kid and brought him back home to his parents.

The rest of the weekend we took walks, swam and had campfires. I remember while we were out walking, we came upon an old abandoned camp. We got in through the window, and the camp had been vandalized already. There were very old photographs and items all over the camp that we made up stories to go along with.

We had so many laughs and made so many memories for ourselves out of someone else's memories.

Nicky and Michelle did great together from then on. I was happy to have so many great friends all together. We all swore we'd be the best of friends forever.

Chapter 48

DRIVING AND HITCHHIKING

I WENT OUT TO DO the test for my driver's license right after my sixteenth birthday in December 1978. I practiced driving a bit between the house and the road and on the camp road on occasion, so I thought I knew everything I needed to know about driving.

I walked into the Ministry of Transportation with my mother. I wrote the test and did fine on the written part. The police officer took me out to test my actual driving skills. Apparently, I was not very good. When I brought him back to the ministry, he was white in the face, my mom said, and he looked scared. He shook his head at my mom and said, "She's not ready to be driving!"

After I failed the test, Mom got me enrolled in a driver's education program. I realized by the time I finished the course that there were many, many things I didn't know about driving the first time around. The second time, I would be prepared.

Mom and I went back to the ministry to try for the license again. The same police officer was there, and when he saw me, he asked another policeman to please take me for my test. This time, the police officer gave my mom a thumbs up, indicating that I had passed and done very well.

I was so happy to have a driver's license. Now I could borrow Mom and Dad's car and go to Espanola by myself to pick up my girlfriends for dances and parties and sleepovers.

One time I borrowed Brenda's old Nova to go to a dance in Espanola, at the high school. Brenda was working at the hotel, so she wouldn't miss it, but she wanted it back by 2:30 a.m. when she was finished working.

I told her I would wash it and detail it to repay her for the use. She agreed.

I drove by myself and met the gang of girls at the school. The dance was a blast, and afterward, I drove all the girls home and headed back to Nairn to bring the car back to my sister.

On the way home, Brenda's old car, with its rusty, sharp rims, had a tire blow out. I had to get off the road about 15 miles east of Nairn. The highway was dead at one o'clock in the morning. With no phone or houses nearby, I had to figure out what to do next.

I'd never been anywhere alone like this at this time of night. I felt vulnerable as a 16-year-old girl out in the middle of nowhere. I had to lock up the car and start walking toward town.

A car drove by and stopped on the highway ahead. It backed up to where I was, and the driver asked if I was okay.

"Yeah," I said. "I just got a flat on my car back there, and I have to get to Nairn."

There were two young men in the car. They told me that they would be happy to give me a lift. They were going through Nairn to get to Sudbury anyway. They were nice enough guys, I figured. They stopped the car and I got into the backseat.

They drove me all the way to the hotel where Brenda worked. They came in with me, and we explained to Brenda what had happened. Brenda was worried that if Mom and Dad found out I hitchhiked home because of her old Nova, she would be in trouble too.

She bought the two guys each a drink to thank them. The bar was ready to close, and the two gentlemen had yet to drive to Sudbury. They said good-bye, hugged me, thanked Brenda for the beer and went on their way.

Brenda knew I had no choice but to hitchhike after I'd told her what happened with her car. She kept telling me how lucky I was to have gotten a ride from people who were good at that time of night. Brenda explained that a young girl like me should not be hitchhiking. "It is very fortunate that you didn't get yourself raped!" she said.

I did end up telling Mom the truth, and she just told me to use her car from then on. Dad ended up putting new rims and tires on the Nova for Brenda's safety.

Chapter 49

A WESTRUCK

MICHELLE AND NICKY AND I had a great gang of girls to hang out with. We were all happy and getting along so well—until that autumn, when I got a phone call.

Mom answered and handed me the phone. "It's for you, it's a boy!" she whispered.

I answered, "Hello?"

It was Nicky's ex-boyfriend, Dale, calling my house, asking for me.

I figured he wanted to know something about Nicky. I thought he must be missing her and afraid to call her himself. I was so surprised when he said the reason he was calling was to ask me to go to a party with him next weekend.

I was awestruck; I didn't even think Dale had noticed me. I surely had never felt him look at me that way when he was with Nicky.

I kept asking him, "Are you sure you meant to call me?"

He'd laugh and say, "Yes, I'm sure. I really always liked you!"

We talked on the telephone for a long time that night. I mentioned Nicky, and he told me that there was never anything real or important going on between her and him. He reminded me that they had stopped seeing each other months ago and reassured me that Nicky would likely be okay with him taking me out by now. He told me he'd always thought I was cute, even while he was seeing Nicky. But it wouldn't have been right to ask me out until some time had passed.

The party that he asked me to go to with him was at his sister's house in Nicky's hometown, Webwood. He would pick me up and bring me back home after it. I was so excited that he had asked *me*.

When I hung up, Mom could see that I was excited. I asked her if I could go to a party next Saturday night with a date. Mom said yes, it was fine. I didn't tell Mom who Dale was—Nicky's old boyfriend. I figured that it was really irrelevant for Mom to know.

It was all the way back in the previous school year when Nicky and Dale had broken up. Maybe she wouldn't mind if I dated him, since she didn't want him anymore.

I guess I hadn't really thought enough about it, because boy, was I wrong! Nicky was angry with me and hurt that I had agreed to go out with Dale. She couldn't believe that I could do that to her. I told her, "He called me!" I started to tell her how it all came about. She didn't want to know any of the details. She just turned and walked away from me.

I'm sure that Nicky wished she had never met me. I thought of how she trusted me with all of the intimate details between her and Dale, not so long ago. I felt bad, but not bad enough to turn it all around and tell him I didn't want to go out with him. I think I was too flattered that he'd even picked me to take out after going out with Nicky. She was so much prettier and more mature than I was.

I had only been on a real date once before, with a boy from school named Larry. He asked me to go to the movies with him, and my mom and dad had to drive me there and pick me up. Larry and I sat in the movie watching and not knowing what to say to each other. He never tried to kiss me, put his arm around me or anything.

Larry and I saw each other at school, and after the movie we considered ourselves boyfriend and girlfriend. We had nothing in common, except for the fact that all of our friends were going steady with somebody. We held hands and walked together at lunch hour.

I broke up with him, from whatever you'd call what we were involved in together, just before Christmas. I didn't want a gift from him, and I didn't want to have to get him a gift. I was not ready to be buying boy's stuff for a boy I hardly knew. The thought of getting him something that he might think was stupid was terrifying. I was happy to be free of the obligation, although I did kind of miss holding his hand at lunch hour.

I always liked Alan and was smitten when I would see him in school. Now and then he would follow me up and down the halls at lunch hour and joke around with me. I could not get over the age gap and the feeling that I was too old for him. If I could have gotten past that, I would have gone out with him in a heartbeat.

Sometimes I really hated myself for avoiding Alan. I felt catty and two-faced, but I didn't want to hurt him. However, I would never completely stop thinking about him. He'd get a girlfriend and I'd feel jealous. I'd get a boyfriend and he'd obviously be jealous. We always seemed happiest when we were both without partners.

I realized that I wanted to be with Alan, but as soon as I could be with him I was terrified of the reality of it and would start avoiding him. I would dream about Alan at night. I would look for him on breaks in the lunchroom or the gym. I didn't want to have him as a boyfriend and lose him as a friend. It was easier not to risk our friendship by dating him and possibly losing him completely.

Dale, however, was an older man. He was much more mature than any boy who had ever asked me out. I figured that if Nicky had him as a boyfriend, then I was just lucky to even have him look twice at me.

Chapter 50

FIRST DATE

DALE PICKED ME UP FROM my house in his father's Buick. He came in to meet my parents. Then he and I left for the party at his sister's house. I thought he smelled so good and looked so nice. I was infatuated with him.

There were not a whole lot of people at his sister's party, but we made the best of it. He served me a glass of rum and Coke. I'd asked for rum when he'd offered me a drink of alcohol. I didn't want to seem immature or like I didn't drink. I didn't really know a lot about different drinks, but my sister always drank rum and Coke.

I had two drinks, and that was my limit. I knew I was feeling the alcohol and it was fun, but I didn't want to make a fool of myself.

Dale and I sat on the couch in a quiet room next to his sister and her friends. The others were partying in the game room just up a floor. We sat close together on the couch and talked about everything and anything. It felt like we'd known each other forever.

My feet started to get cold, and Dale picked them up and put them into his lap. He rubbed them to warm them up. The touch of his hands on my feet felt so nice. We cuddled for a bit while we talked and then he kissed me. He was a real gentleman about it too. He asked if it would be okay to kiss me, and of course my reply was yes.

We kissed every now and then when the feeling overcame us. We talked until midnight, and then, unfortunately, I realized and told Dale that I should probably get home soon. He agreed and said it was probably getting late, and it was time, although he would rather sit and talk with me all night.

In the car on the way home, he asked me to sit closer to him so he could hold my hand. Everything felt so right. We both agreed that we'd enjoyed each other's company, and we'd like to see each other again. When we got to my house, he kissed me goodnight in the car, and we said good-bye.

I couldn't believe all of the feelings I was having for him already after just one date. I went upstairs to go to bed and said goodnight to Mom and Dad, who were already in bed but waiting up for me. I walked into my room with a big smile on my face because I thought it was the happiest night of my life.

Bright and early the next day, Dale called me. We'd really hit it off. He thought so too. We started talking on the phone to one another every night before bedtime. He'd call me long distance "just to hear my voice," he'd say. We'd plan our weekends together.

When I went back to school, I realized that my friend Nicky was gone for good. I tried to say hello and chat with her, but she was obviously ignoring me and had no intentions on reconciling. I saw Michelle on my breaks and at lunch. I told Michelle about Dale, and she thought that my going out with him was a big mistake. She didn't blame Nicky for not wanting to talk to me.

I thought that Nicky would have a change of heart when she realized that Dale was meant to be with me. I didn't care what Michelle thought, although I was happy she wasn't ignoring me. She'd ask me over on the weekends, and I had to tell her I was busy because Dale and I had plans already. She really didn't like Dale taking me over completely. Michelle was upset that Dale was all I would eat, sleep or breathe anymore.

I ended up leaving Michelle behind as well for the rest of Grade 11, to be obsessed with Dale. I waited hours, minutes and seconds by the phone for him to call. Talking and listening, waiting and wanting passionately to be with him, it could never be soon enough that I could see him.

My mom became a little protective, wanting to know where I was going with Dale and who would be there with us. She made sure that I knew to be careful.

On occasion, Mom and Dad would allow me to have Dale sleep over in the spare room. They thought he was a nice kid. They didn't seem to mind our dating each other. I never really got the feeling that they were happy about it, though, either. I was ready to go anywhere with him, any time he would come to get me.

Dale and I started necking and cuddling all the time. He asked me to go steady with him, and I was ecstatic. He gave me his initial ring to wear as a symbol of our friendship. I thought he and I would totally and truly be in love forever.

We'd talk every day and plan every minute we could to be together. It wasn't long after "the feeling-up stage" that we started talking about having sex together. I knew it was coming. I had even started thinking about it myself. We talked about it, and I told him that I wouldn't be ready to make love unless I could be absolutely safe from becoming pregnant.

Besides Brenda, I'd had my close cousin, Colette, Aunty Fern's daughter, get pregnant the year before at age 14. She had a baby girl and had to quit school and get a place of her own. She was very unhappy, and the baby was a whole lot of work. I knew that this was not something I wanted to have happen to me now, not yet anyway. Dale agreed with me that we should wait to be safe. I told him I would go on the pill, and we could start to plan our first time together.

I went to my mom to ask her about going on the birth-control pill. She was appalled. She said, "No, I'm not going to help you go on the pill." She added, "Going on the pill doesn't mean it's okay to have sex, either!"

I tried to explain to her that I was going to have sex regardless of what she wanted. I was a woman now, and it was going to happen sooner or later. She would just have to get used to the idea. All of my friends were already having sex, and when she was my age, she was married to Dad with a baby on the way.

I knew that sex was going to happen whether Mom could handle it or not. She still disagreed with the whole concept of it and would not give me her consent to go on the pill. I had to go ahead on my own and make an appointment to see my doctor in Espanola during my lunch hour at school. My doctor gave me a prescription for the pill without even questioning me. He was very understanding. He answered all of the questions I had. He told me not to trust the pill alone for at least three months, because it would take at least that long to be 90 percent safe.

My mother, on the other hand, didn't talk much to me anymore. She never spoke to me about it again. She never asked me if I'd gotten the pill or was taking it. It took about two weeks until she would even look at me again.

The pill made my period very irregular. Sometimes I'd bleed one day. Sometimes I'd bleed for a week and a half. Dale agreed to wait the three months with me, without putting pressure on me.

We both looked forward to our first time with anticipation. He'd never had sex either. It was like waiting for Christmas. I only got to see Dale on weekends, so it seemed like forever in between visits.

Dale picked me up from school the weekend of Valentine's Day. Coincidentally, our three-month waiting period was finally over. We had asked my mom if I could go with him to stay at his sister and her husband's house for the weekend. Mom was okay with that. She figured his sister would keep her eye on us. We'd been there before. All parents must be as protective as she was.

We spent the evening with Dale's sister and her family, and then they all turned in to bed for the night and we were left alone. We were both excited and anxious. We knew tonight would be the night, and we planned our secret rendezvous.

I was going to sleep in the basement bedroom, and Dale was going to sleep upstairs on the couch. Dale brought me downstairs to tuck me in, and when he turned on the light, I was so surprised. He had decorated the room with teddy bears and a heart-shaped box of chocolates and flowers. He'd made our first night together such a wonderful romantic surprise.

We started cuddling on the bed, and soon we had all of our clothes off and were making love. It was a very special night for me. I figured this meant that we were going to be together forever. I was so pleased that he'd had the patience to wait for me to be safe from pregnancy. I was so in love with him.

Chapter 51

LOVE HURTS

DALE HAD BEEN SAVING HIS money from a job he was working at. He bought a van shortly after our weekend at his sister's. We went to Dale's dad's house and stayed in the van in the driveway at night. His dad was cool with us sleeping together.

Dale and I spent many days and nights in the van together making love and talking. He got a Polaroid camera, and we took some naked pictures of each other. He kept some for himself, and I took some and put them in my diary at home.

One day when I got home from school, my mother was sitting in the living room, and when I yelled, "Hi, I'm home," she ignored me completely. I ran up the stairs to ask her what was wrong and find out why she didn't say "hi" back. Mom got up and walked away from me without a word. I followed her and asked her again what was wrong.

"Go see in your room" is all that Mom said. She continued to disregard me.

I walked up to my room to see what she was sending me there for. Everything seemed in order. But there was a handwritten note on my bed from my mother.

In the note she wrote, "Poochie, I am so disgusted with you, I can't believe the things that you have been doing. I've read your diary, and I am so disappointed in you. You cannot imagine the disgust I felt when I read and saw everything that you had done. I can't even look at you, let alone call you my daughter. I don't know what to say other than I don't want to see your face or talk to you ever again."

I fell onto my bed, devastated. I couldn't believe she would break into my jewellery box and read my diary. I didn't think she even knew it was there.

All those stupid naked pictures and all those times I'd written about making love with Dale. I didn't know why Mom would have wanted to read my diary. Why was she so curious? How was I going to live without my mom?

I couldn't believe this was happening, I went back down the stairs to ask Mom why she broke into my jewellery box, but she was gone. I felt lost and in distress. I didn't know what to do. I felt sick. I went back upstairs and lay down on my bed.

I heard the door again later, and it was Mom and Dad. Mom was crying when I came downstairs to talk to her. She still wouldn't look at me or speak to me. My dad looked at me with a very confused, hurt look.

"When is she going to talk to me again?" I said.

"Never, you're not anything but a little whore!" she screamed.

Dad motioned me to just go away, and he went to comfort Mom and calm her down. I left the room and waited around the corner listening for any words, but none came. The TV went on and Dad sat down to watch it. Mom sat in her rocking chair staring out into space.

I went back up to my room. I couldn't really understand what my mom was going through. All I know is that I felt embarrassed and betrayed. I was angry and sorry and sad. There were so many emotions going through my head.

I hardly slept at all that night. I kept waking up thinking I was dreaming. I'd never seen Mom act like this before. I felt numb and scared. Somehow I drifted off to sleep.

Mom continued to ignore me throughout the week. I walked over to Brenda's house and told her what had happened. I really needed to talk to someone. Brenda was cleaning her apartment. She sat down at the kitchen table and said to me, "Mom was wrong to have done what she did."

But that doesn't help me, I thought.

Brenda put her arm around me and said, "Mom is angry right now, but she will get over this."

I wanted to believe Brenda, but somehow, I felt this situation was not just a little upset like any other little upset. I did feel better knowing that Brenda was there to talk to.

Brenda came over to the house with me and told Mom that she had no business breaking into my diary. Mom ignored her and wouldn't talk to Brenda either. Mom was not going apologize. She was not going to let go of the disappointment and disgust she held for me. She simply didn't care if I lived or died.

I was thankful to have Brenda there to try to help me. Things were never going to be the same without my mom. I felt such a void that I couldn't eat, sleep or do anything. I wished myself dead. I knew that I had disappointed Mom and let her down. It upset me greatly to have hurt her so much. I missed her.

I thought that eventually Mom would be okay with my having had sex, especially since I was so careful and in love with Dale. I spent the next while of my life going to school and coming home to Mom's cold shoulder. I was lost and alone without her. Dad stood by her no matter what, so he wasn't really available for me either. I felt numb and helpless. I didn't know how I could go on.

Dale called, and I told him about what was going on in my house. He didn't think it was so serious. "She didn't kick you out, did she?" he asked.

"No, but she won't even look at me," I said.

He just told me not to worry about it and carry on with my life, that I didn't need a mommy anymore anyway. I thought he was kind of cold with me. Maybe it was because his mother had died when he was so young. Maybe he was jealous of my relationship with her.

We talked a while about the upcoming weekend, and then we said good-bye and hung up. I didn't feel like he was someone I could talk to right now.

It was difficult to live in the same house with Mom ignoring me. I took the diary and all of the pictures and threw the whole pile of things out in the garbage. I walked up to Mom in the living room.

I told her that I had destroyed everything. I was hoping that getting rid of the evidence would make all of the problems disappear.

"It doesn't make any difference, you can't take back all of the things you have done," she said. "You're disgusting!"

My head fell and I moped around. I went back up to my room to be alone. I was mad at myself, I was mad at her, and I didn't care about anything else anymore. I walked around like zombie for the rest of the week. I looked forward to the weekend, when I would see Dale again.

I always used to ask Mom if it was okay to go away on the weekends. I didn't know if I should stay or go with Dale to his sister's house. I didn't even know how to leave the house without asking Mom and making sure she was okay with things. I thought I would give her the courtesy of still asking if she minded my going with Dale this weekend.

Mom just shrugged and said, "Do whatever you want. I don't care about you anymore. Dad and I won't even be here this weekend."

I just walked away, feeling empty. "I might as well go," I said.

Chapter 52

FOUL PLAY

DALE PICKED ME UP IN the van, and we went to his other sister's home. She was married and had two kids and lived just east of Sudbury. She and her husband offered us the bedroom over their garage for the night. They seemed genuinely excited to have us over.

We had a nice day with his sister and brother-in-law and their family. It helped to be away from home and from my mom's ignoring me. I was able to forget and to function and have a bit of fun.

We ate a wonderful barbequed meal together on the deck. We had dinner with wine. I had a really nice time with his sister. I liked her and her husband, and I could tell that they liked me too. His sister said that if Dale loved me, so did she.

In the evening, Dale's brother-in-law brought out more wine, and we all had another glass. Dale was sitting at my feet on the carpet, leaning on the foot of the couch. I was sitting on one end of the couch, and Dale's brother-in-law was at the other. His sister was in the easy chair next to the window, and Dale was soon on the floor sleeping.

We were having a nice conversation when his sister noticed that Dale was asleep. She got up, stretched and yawned, and said she was ready for bed. She said she was going to check on the children and would see us in the morning, and to have a good night. She gave her husband a kiss and left.

Suddenly I felt uncomfortable. I wished Dale would wake up and take me out to the garage to be alone and go to bed.

After Dale's sister was gone, his brother-in-law took out a joint of marijuana and lit it. I didn't want to seem like a stick-in-the-mud, so when he offered it to me, I took it and took a puff of it. I choked a bit and didn't like it. I felt like I'd been kind enough joining him; I didn't need any more. I had never smoked pot before. I had only ever watched Brian and his friends do it.

Dale's brother-in-law moved to the middle of the couch, and he was sitting directly beside me, so close our legs were touching. I could feel his breath on me when he spoke.

Suddenly he slid his hand underneath my bottom on the couch. He took my other hand and put it on his crotch. I didn't know what to do. I was shocked. I felt so violated and trapped. I didn't want to make a fuss, because I would ruin the whole day for everybody. These were Dale's relatives, and I didn't want to disappoint Dale or his sister.

I looked at the brother-in-law with confusion. I took my hand back and tried to pretend that I didn't understand what he was trying to do. I got up and said, "I have to go to the bathroom."

I walked briskly into the bathroom, and I stayed there for a long time. I finally got my courage up and made a decision as to what to do. I came out of the bathroom. I was not going to sit down again. I was going to wake Dale up and take him to the garage to bed.

Dale's brother-in-law blocked the doorway to the living room. I could not get back in to wake up Dale up. He walked out in front of me as I was coming down the hall.

He grabbed my hand and started pulling me and trying to kiss me, saying, "You want it, you know you do!"

He was planning to take me outside to the garage. He was trying to drag me out the front door when I slipped and got my hand free. I ran back to Dale and shook him to wake up.

Dale was startled. "What's up?" he asked.

"Get up," I said to him. "It's time for bed!"

I tried to keep calm. I felt better now that he was awake. But he just laid there and wanted to go back to sleep. I had to pinch him to show him I meant business. He gave me a look as if to say, *What the heck are you doing?*

I just wanted to get out of that house and not cause any trouble. I told Dale that I was ready for bed. I asked him to please get up and take me to where we were going to sleep.

"Yah sure," he answered, still kind of dazed.

He was not getting the hint that I felt danger. I took his hand and helped him up off of the floor. I held onto his hand tightly, and we walked right past his brother-in-law. "G'night," Dale yelled.

We got outside the front door and went into the garage. I made sure not to meet eyes with the brother-in-law again.

I tried to talk to Dale the minute we were alone. "Your brother-in-law was trying to feel me up on the couch, and then he grabbed my hand and was trying to pull me into the garage," I cried.

Dale looked at me in disbelief.

I explained to Dale, "Your brother-in-law put his hand right under my butt while we were sitting on the couch, and he started feeling me up. You were sleeping, right there in front of us! He put my hand on his crotch!" I cried.

Dale didn't look concerned, because he didn't believe what I had just told him. He made light of it. He said, "You've had too much to drink," and he led me up to the garage bedroom where we were going to sleep.

"We can talk about it in the morning," he yawned. "I'm tired right now." Dale did not touch me, he did not hold me and tell me not to worry and that everything would be all right. I thought I must be in the Twilight Zone.

I walked down to Dale's van once he had fallen asleep, which he did as soon as his head hit the pillow. I contemplated driving myself home. The keys were not in the ignition, so that stopped that thought in its tracks. I couldn't just steal his van anyway. I leaned back against the door of the van looking up at the stars.

Could I be making a big deal of nothing? I did not want this to be happening. Dale was not understanding or not caring that I did not feel safe. Wasn't it important for me to feel safe?

I questioned myself. What did I do to bring this on? I didn't think I did anything but try to be friendly to the whole family. I never even thought of Dale's brother-in-law in a sexual way. I never did anything to make him feel like I was interested in him that way.

I kept thinking . . . at dinner, I had talked about how in love I was with Dale. Why would he think that I would want to have sex with him? How did the night end up like this? Well, it didn't much matter how often I analyzed it, Dale was not going to do anything about it right now. Maybe he was drunk. I hoped that would be his excuse for belittling me.

He will sleep on it and take it less kindly in the morning. I'm sure I matter to him, he loves me, I kept reassuring myself.

I went back up the stairs into the garage loft. I lay down beside Dale. I watched him sleep, so soundly, without a care in the world. I was dumbstruck and in a state of disbelief. I would feel rage coming over me, and I would sit up. I started thinking and wondering what I could do to make the night go by more quickly. I lay there waiting for the morning. Dozing off and on, I imagined that maybe I had been dreaming this whole scenario. I'd wake back up every now and then and feel anxiety come over me.

Each time I awoke, I'd realize that it was not a dream, and I tried to figure out what I was going to do about it. Dale and I were leaving the next day. I was going to have to get through breakfast with the family now. I drifted off for a longer period at some point and woke up to find that Dale had gotten up and left me there.

Still lying on the covers in the same clothes that I had on the night before, I felt colder than ever and so alone. I could feel tears coming, and I held them in. I stood up, straightened my clothes and ran my hand down my hair to make sure I looked presentable. I took a deep breath and walked down the stairs and back into the house to find Dale.

He was sitting at the kitchen table. I sat down in the empty chair beside him. The whole family was in the kitchen.

"Good morning," they all bellowed.

"Good morning," I said quietly back.

I kept my head down and kept looking over at Dale to see what his expression was. Dale looked normal, undisturbed. He never brought anything up about the previous night.

I figured he would probably rather just get breakfast over with, and we'd talk about it alone on the way home. I felt like I was in a trance. I was quiet and reserved. Dale proceeded to chitchat like nothing had happened. The conversation was all about their family and the kids, the fact that they were renovating their house, and a lot of other things that were so trivial to me at that moment.

The thoughts in my head were on pause. I could not even speak or gesture. The brother-in-law knew something was wrong with me. He knew what it was, too. He would make a joke, and I would ignore him. He was trying to avoid talking about last night, by any means. I think he must have figured I'd just let it go.

Somehow, we got through breakfast all together. Dale said, after finishing his coffee, "We should probably go. We've got to get Bev all the way back to Nairn." We got up and started toward the door. I'm sure I appeared to be in a rush.

Dale added, "We had a great time. Thanks for everything."

His sister and brother-in-law stood up from the table and came toward us. We had to get through hugging and saying good-bye, and we finally left the house to get into the van. I'm sure his sister thought I was mentally unstable. She must have wondered what was going on with me. Last night I was fun and outgoing, and this morning I made no eye contact and was not even courteous. I'm sure her husband knew why.

I was very angry, and I made sure Dale knew as soon as we got out of the driveway.

Dale just looked at me as if he was not happy with my behaviour. He said, "Why are you doing this? Weren't they nice enough to you?" He went on, "What is it with girls like you? You're just not happy unless everyone is hot for you?"

I was appalled. Dale really did not believe me, nor did he want to. I sat in tears and grief and bewilderment. We never said another word to each other all the way to my house, which took us about an hour to get to.

Dale got out of the van when we got to my house and came around to my side of the van and opened the door for me. I got out. He slammed the van door behind me and just walked around and got back into the driver's seat. He sped out of the driveway, leaving me standing there.

I took out my house key and opened the door to the empty house.

Chapter 53

RELATIONSHIP ARRESTED

MY MOM AND DAD HAD gone out of town for the weekend. When I got into the house, I fell to my knees and broke down crying hysterically. I was sick to my stomach. I wanted to die. I felt like I was going out of my mind. I walked around the house in a state of emptiness, loneliness, crying and screaming.

I went up to my bedroom and lay down on my bed. I felt like I was lost. I didn't belong in my own house anymore. Mom had disowned me. Dale didn't love me. I contemplated taking a handful of pills or slitting my wrists.

I didn't really want to die; I just couldn't live like this anymore. I cried until my eyes were swollen shut, and I had no more tears to cry. I got under the blankets and just wanted to hide away from the world. I closed my eyes. A welcome feeling of exhaustion came over me, and I fell into a deep sleep.

I was awakened by the telephone ringing. I jumped up and ran to answer it. I was hoping it was Dale.

It was Dale's brother-in-law, calling me to say I shouldn't have told Dale the things that I did. Dale had gone back to his house to confront him in front of his wife and kids. He yelled into the phone at me, "Dale said that you accused me of trying to have sex with you!"

I guessed that his wife was in the room with him, which was why he was denying it

Dale's brother-in-law told me that I had caused quite a disturbance to the whole family, and he was going to take me to court for slander. I was terrified. I felt like I was in a tunnel going further and further down.

When he hung up, I started crying again. *What have I done, why is this happening to me?* I said to myself through tears.

The phone rang again. It was Dale's sister this time, yelling and crying into the phone and saying I was nothing but a lying little tramp. She said they were not going to let me say things like that about their family. I was nothing but a bitch and a home wrecker. She was claiming that I was harassing them. She denied that what I had told Dale could have happened. She and her husband had a loving marriage; why would he even attempt to do something like that with his whole family in the same house?

She threatened me by saying that they were not going to just let this ride, they would be taking legal action against me. I just listened and said nothing. I felt scared and confused and did not know what to say.

They called me again and again, yelling and cursing and accusing me of being nothing but a troublemaker.

Mom and Dad came home that evening. I heard the front door close as they came into the house. Mom came upstairs, opened my bedroom door, walked in and sat down on the side of my bed. She saw that my eyes were glued closed from crying. I was slobbering and very emotional. I think at that point she was worried about my well-being.

It felt so good to see her concerned face looking at me, but it also made me cry even more. I broke down and begged, "Please Mom, just love me. I didn't mean to hurt you. I love you." I grabbed her and hugged her and said, "I never would do anything to purposefully hurt you. I can't live without you. I'd rather die!"

I also knew I had to tell her and Dad the rest of the story. The phone had been ringing so often, I was sure Mom or Dad would end up picking up the receiver the next time it rang and hear someone yelling into it. I felt like there was no way out. They needed to know that this insane state of mine came from a whole lot of things going on. That I had reached rock bottom.

The words with tears just spewed out of my mouth with sobbing and gasping breaths.

Mom could see I was at a breaking point. She knew that I was frustrated and very depressed. I could tell that she was afraid of what I might do to myself. She was afraid because I was afraid, and I showed it.

"The next time they call, I will answer the phone," she said.

This whole last month seemed like such a foreign and strange experience. *But what happened?* I wondered. While Mom and I were apart this weekend, everything had changed.

The unravelling world seemed to have wound itself back up a bit. It was like something had turned Mom upside down and shook her. Did she really forgive me? Did she love me again?

Then the phone rang.

Mom answered the phone without saying a word and listened. Dale's brother-in-law started in on Mom, thinking he was talking to me. He was telling her that she was a bitch and that they were going to take her to court for slandering their name.

When he stopped, Mom said to him, "Are you finished?"

The brother-in-law was quiet when he realized it was not me that he was yelling at on the phone. The world was quiet, and I waited to hear what Mom would say to him.

Finally she spoke. "You bastard," Mom said. "You go ahead and take her to court for slander. We'll take you to court for attempted rape!"

My mom stayed on the line waiting for a response. All you could hear was a click and the dial tone. They never called my house again.

Mom told me, "Don't you worry. He won't dare follow through with any of his accusations. He's got much more working against him than for him, by the sounds of what you told me. Giving alcohol to a minor, having marijuana in the house. He won't bother you again."

I was so relieved to think that maybe this too would all pass.

My mother was my hero, and I can't even explain the strength she gave me and the love I felt for her at that moment. I hugged her and kissed her. I wanted her to forgive me.

I told Mom that I missed her so much, and that I would be good from now on. "I will do anything to have my mom back," I told her.

Mom said, "This relationship with Dale is over. What kind of man loves you and does not trust you, and is not there for you when you need him? He is not good enough to be with you!"

I couldn't figure out how I had gotten so far into this relationship without seeing things more clearly. I was angry, and I felt like I had been so naïve. I felt resentment building. I started thinking that I should hate Dale for this. My safety was important, after all!

I bounced back and forth between hating him and missing him. Wanting to forgive him and wanting to be forgiven by him.

I thought eventually he would come to his senses. I thought he would shake his head, wake up and call me to say he was sorry or to ask me to please forgive him because he loved me. But he didn't call, and I started to feel like maybe our whole relationship had been a game for him. He'd probably thought I was a sucker. Now that he'd used me and abused me, he would just forget me.

My imagination was tearing at me constantly. Did I really want him back? Maybe I just wanted the opportunity to have him beg for my forgiveness, just to be able to tell him, "No, I don't forgive you, and we are through!"

But Dale did not call or write or drop by, and I had a lot to recover from after that. I hated myself for having done those photographs for him. I'd never know where the pictures might end up.

I hated myself. I hated that I believed him when he told me he loved me. I wondered if I was his first and only love. I hurt for having given up my friends for him. It was going to be hard to forgive myself for the mess I had gotten myself into.

I was so very depressed; I could not see this pain ever coming to an end. I wished it to be just a dream, every morning when I woke up. I wanted Dale back, and I hated him. I had to keep myself away from the phone. It was like an addiction. I'd be waiting for him to call me, or I'd be battling with my own mind to stop myself from calling him.

I knew I had to get over this great ordeal to become whole again. But I hadn't a clue as to how I was going to do that.

Mom and I were good, and that was truly all that mattered. I reminded myself that I had promised Mom I would not go back to Dale.

Dad was happy too, and things were finally starting to feel like the old normal that home used to feel like . . . except for the painfully numb feeling of having had someone abandon me. It was tough love being accused of being a liar and a whore and fighting the feelings of love, hate, resentment and denial that kept running through my head.

If I could have forgotten the last year, it would have been so much easier. My bed became my favourite place to be, asleep my favourite state of mind. Time was what it was going to take, and I wanted to sleep that time away.

Chapter 54

MOM'S GUEST AGAIN

M OM AND DAD DECIDED TO take me up to the cottage for the last weekend of summer before school started, hoping to rouse me from my depression over Dale. There was no telephone at the cottage, but there was the beach and the sunshine, the canoe and the fish, and we all thought it would be good for me to get away from the phone, the waiting, the wondering and the pain from the rut that I felt that I was in.

It was nice to be at the cottage. It was a change of scenery, which was a good change. I was still feeling alone and depressed. I felt as if a huge part of me had curled up and died. I had no idea how to get over this lonely, empty feeling.

Mom was feeling bad for me in my lonely state, so she took the liberty of putting together a surprise for me. She left me up at the cottage and drove into town.

I sat on the end of the dock for hours that day and looked out at the sunset, dreaming of the past and of the future. Trying to forget the moment and remember what life used to be like, before Dale. I wanted to remember the way it used to feel to just be me.

I was still sitting on the dock by myself when Mom returned. I felt a tap on my shoulder and turned around. It was Mom, and she had once again picked up a friend to come back with her and keep me company.

I was so surprised and happy when I saw Michelle. She was smiling and standing behind me with her arms open. I got up and hugged her like she was the long lost teddy bear I had finally found again.

I reminded Mom of this very same incident that had happened so very long ago with Sherry. I told Mom, "Hey, you brought her here, you play with her!"

Mom and I laughed.

Bringing Michelle was the best thing Mom could have done for me. I needed to talk and cry and laugh, and Mom was getting pretty worn out just listening and comforting me. I knew she needed a break.

That was Grade 11 summer vacation. It was a very long tearful summer. I was so grateful to have a friend like Michelle to talk to and start the next school year with.

One thing meant more to me than anything else that summer. It was that I had a mom who really loved me and would stand by me no matter what.

The End

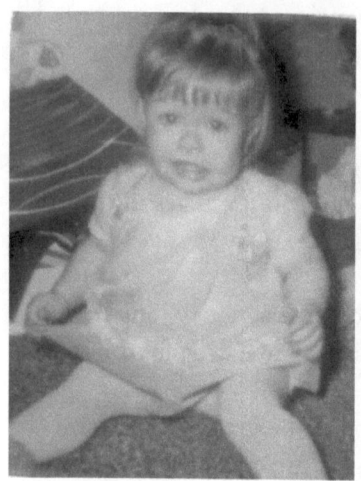

Poochie Marcoux born
December 5th, 1962

Brenda Dad Poochie Brian

Annette Prince Marcoux born
August 20th 1935

Roger Marcoux born
April 2, 1932

Brian Marcoux and Menew

Brenda Marcoux Catholic
ceremony with Dad

Brian Dad and Brenda

Poochie 3 years old

Uncle Ray teaching Poochie to
swim n Brenda

Yvonne Deroy Grandma
Badgerow

Roger Marcoux and work truck

Mom n Brian n Canvas shack

Catholic Church

Dad's brought home
another white car

Billy and I at Grade 8 graduation

Pat Badgerow grade 8 graduation

Mamere Marcoux

Henrys tent at Marcoux reunion

Brian Marcoux age 16 born
February 24 1956

Brenda marcoux age 18, born
September 14, 1953

Scow that crosses the Spanish
River into Nairn

Best Friends girls of
summer80

Poochie Marcoux grade 12

Mother page 4

Family Tree

Grandparents: Hector Marcoux and Aline Proulx, Marcoux
Siblings: Leo, Henry, Bill, Faye, Fern, (my father, Roger), Harvey, Dorelda, Ron, Dennis, Shirley Marcoux

Grandparents: Edward Prince and Yvonne, Deroy Courchesne, Prince, Badgerow, Leduc.
Siblings: Felix, George, Marie Courchesne, Edward, Peter, (my mother, Annette), Margarette Prince, Omer, Ann Badgerow

About the Author

*B*EVERLY ANN MARCOUX JOHNSTON IS married to Scott Allan Johnston. They live on a heritage property on the Niagara Escarpment in Burlington, Ontario, Canada. Beverly has two sons, Dalton and Sam, which she had with Scott and two stepsons of Scott's, Chad and Shane. She and her husband escape the cold northern winters in her condo in Venice, Florida. She is a member and supporter of PERL (Protect the Escarpment Rural Lands) and a volunteer at the Joseph Brant Memorial Hospital HELP (Help the Elder Live Program). She enjoys writing, watercolour painting and creating lamp-work jewellery.